THE GIFT OF CHRISTMAS

Create Ornaments, Floral Arrangements, Gifts & More

The Home Decorating Institute®

CREATIVE
PUBLISHING
international

Copyright © 1996 Creative Publishing international, Inc.
5900 Green Oak Drive Minnetonka, Minnesota 55343 • 1-800-328-3895 • All rights reserved • Printed in U.S.A.

Library of Congress Cataloging-in-Publication Data The gift of Christmas / the Home Decorating Institute. p. cm. — (Arts & crafts for home decorating) Includes index. ISBN 0-86573-389-9 (hardcover) — ISBN 0-86573-390-2 (softcover) 1. Christmas decorations. I. Home Decorating Institute (Minnetonka, Minn.) II. Series.   TT900.C4G47 1996 745.594'12 — dc20   95-50769

CONTENTS

The Gift of Christmas

Decorating the Tree

Around the House

Gift Giving & Cards

To: Carol
From: Mom

THE GIFT OF CHRISTMAS

*Create personalized
holiday decorations and gifts
for your home, family, and friends*

Decorate the tree with handcrafted ornaments like scherenschnitte ornaments, hand-cast paper ornaments, lace doily ornaments, and string ball ornaments. Choose from a layered tree skirt or several other tree skirt ideas.

Carry the holiday spirit throughout the house with decorations like the tiered wood Christmas tree, holiday placemats and napkins, or an elegant floral arrangement. Embellish a wall or mantel with a miniature Christmas tree topped with a bow.

For personalized holiday gifts, make a set of holiday coasters, a log carrier, pinecone kindlers, or a candy wreath. Then discover ways to creatively wrap your custom-made gifts and find unique ideas for personalized gift tags and cards.

Decorating
The Tree

STRING BALL ORNAMENTS

Oversized string balls filled with nothing but air seem to magically keep their shape. An ornament is created by wrapping a balloon with string and decorative cords or narrow ribbons, then applying a liquid fabric stiffener and allowing it to dry. When the balloon is popped and removed, the stiffened string ball can be decorated with ribbons and other embellishments. Hang the ornaments on the Christmas tree, or arrange them around an evergreen garland on a buffet or mantel.

MATERIALS

- Round latex balloons, in desired sizes.
- Liquid fabric stiffener.
- Foam applicator.
- Wrapping materials, such as string, metallic cord, narrow braid, and narrow ribbon.
- Clothespins, dowel 3/8" (1 cm) or smaller in diameter, and deep cardboard box, for suspending wet balloon.
- Metallic cord, for hanger; large-eyed needle.
- Ribbon, for bows.
- Embellishments, such as glitter, sequins, and confetti, optional.

HOW TO MAKE A STRING BALL ORNAMENT

1 Inflate balloon to desired size; knot end. Grasp balloon by the knot; apply thin layer of liquid fabric stiffener to entire surface of balloon, using foam applicator.

2 Wrap end of string loosely around base of knot. Wrap string around balloon and back to knot.

3 Continue to wrap string around the balloon, changing directions gradually; sparsely cover entire surface of balloon. Wrap string loosely around knot; cut string. Apply another layer of fabric stiffener to string.

4 Repeat steps 2 and 3 for each additional layer of wrapping material. Continue to add layers of string until surface of balloon is evenly covered to desired density.

5 Apply generous coat of liquid fabric stiffener over the entire wrapped balloon. Sprinkle with glitter, if desired.

6 Suspend balloon from dowel, using clothespin; prop dowel across opening of deep cardboard box, allowing balloon to drip into box. Allow to dry completely.

7 Pop balloon; loosen any areas of balloon that may stick, using eraser end of pencil. Pull deflated balloon out of the ball through hole left by balloon knot at top. Remove any remaining residue between strings with eraser end of pencil or a pin.

9 Insert ribbons into same holes as cord; tie into bows. Embellish ornament as desired.

8 Attach cord at top of ball, using large-eyed needle; insert needle into hole left by balloon knot, and exit through any space, about ½" (1.3 cm) away. Knot ends of cord to form loop for hanging.

SCHERENSCHNITTE ORNAMENTS & GARLANDS

Simple folding and cutting techniques turn ordinary paper into beautiful ornaments. The German craft of scherenschnitte (shear-en-shnit-tah), or scissors' cuttings, produces an intricate paper filigree that can be displayed as a single, flat ornament or a garland of repeated motifs. Two identical scherenschnitte pieces can be made and sewn together down the center for a three-dimensional ornament. Several patterns for each style are given on page 124. Ornaments can be antiqued, if desired, or painted with watercolor paints. For added sparkle, glitter may be applied to the ornament.

Choose art papers that have a sharp edge when cut. Parchment papers are particularly suitable for scherenschnitte, due to their strength and ability to accept stain or watercolors. Scissors with short, sharp, pointed blades are necessary for the intricate work of scherenschnitte. Tiny detail cutting on the interior of the design is easier to do with a mat knife and cutting surface.

Three-dimensional ornament *is created by stitching two identical symmetrical designs together through the center. You can also make single ornaments or a garland as shown opposite.*

HOW TO MAKE A SINGLE SCHERENSCHNITTE ORNAMENT

MATERIALS

- Tracing paper.
- Art paper.
- Graphite paper, for transferring design; removable tape; scrap of corrugated cardboard.
- Scissors with short, sharp, pointed blades.
- Mat knife and cutting surface.
- Needle; thread, for hanger.
- Instant coffee and cotton-tipped swab, for antiquing, optional.
- Watercolor paints and glitter, optional.

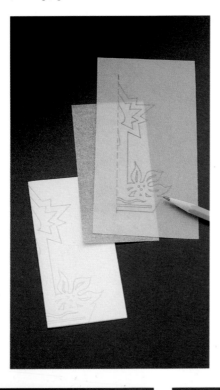

1 Cut a piece of art paper larger than the pattern dimensions (page 124); for a symmetrical design, fold paper in half, right sides together. Trace pattern onto tracing paper. Transfer the design from tracing paper to wrong side of folded art paper, using graphite paper; align the dotted line on design to fold of art paper.

2 Tape folded art paper to cutting surface, placing the tape in area outside design. Cut out interior shapes, using mat knife; begin with shapes nearest fold, and work toward cut edges of paper. Make any small holes by punching through paper with a needle.

3 Remove art paper from cutting surface, and cut outer edge of design with scissors. Open cut design.

4 Press flat with a warm iron. Antique or embellish as desired, using one of the three methods on page 17. Attach thread hanger at center of the ornament, 1/4" (6 mm) from the upper edge, using a hand needle; knot the thread ends.

HOW TO MAKE A THREE-DIMENSIONAL SCHERENSCHNITTE ORNAMENT

1 Follow steps 1 to 4, opposite, for two identical designs, omitting thread hanger. Place the cut designs on top of each other, aligning edges; secure to scrap of corrugated cardboard, using removable tape. Punch holes with pushpin every ¼" (6 mm) along the center fold, through both layers.

2 Thread a needle with 18" (46 cm) length of thread in same color as ornament. Sew in and out of holes from top to bottom of ornament.

3 Turn ornament over, and stitch back up to top hole. Tie the ends of thread together at desired length for hanger. Arrange the ornament sections at right angles to each other.

HOW TO MAKE A SCHERENSCHNITTE GARLAND

1 Cut strip of art paper 11" (28 cm) long and 2¾" (7 cm) wide. Fold in half, wrong sides together, to make 5½" × 4¼" (14 × 10.8 cm) strip. Fold short ends to center fold, right sides together, so the strip is accordion-folded, with wrong side facing out.

2 Trace design for garland (page 124) onto tracing paper. Transfer design from tracing paper to wrong side of folded art paper, using graphite paper; align dotted lines on design to double folded edges of paper.

3 Cut out the design, following steps 2 and 3 for single ornament on page 14. Open out garland. Embellish, if desired, using one of the three methods opposite.

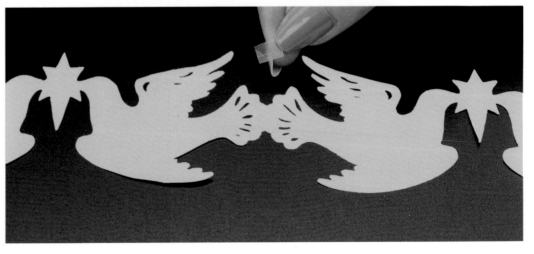

4 Repeat steps 1 to 3 as necessary to make as many garland lengths as desired. Press the garland pieces flat with a warm iron. Join garland lengths with small pieces of tape on wrong side.

HOW TO EMBELLISH SCHERENSCHNITTE ORNAMENTS

Watercolored ornaments. Paint scherenschnitte ornament with watercolor paint and soft brush. Allow to dry; press with warm iron. Repeat on back side.

Glittered ornaments. Apply glue over areas to be glittered, using glue pen. Sprinkle with glitter; shake off the excess. Repeat on back side.

Antiqued ornaments. Mix 1½ teaspoons (7 mL) instant coffee with ½ cup (125 mL) hot water. Apply coffee to outer edge of ornament and around large openings with cotton swab. Allow to dry; press. Repeat on back side.

PAPIER-MÂCHÉ ORNAMENTS

Create easy-to-make papier-mâché ornaments from ready-made forms, available at craft shops. Simply embellish the forms with a variety of paints, beads, or glitter for a shimmering holiday display.

TIPS FOR EMBELLISHING PAPIER-MÂCHÉ ORNAMENTS

Paint the ornaments with aerosol acrylic paint; use pearlescent paint for a lustrous finish.

Apply glitter glue to painted ornaments to create a shimmering raised design.

Embellish the ornaments with beads; secure with craft glue.

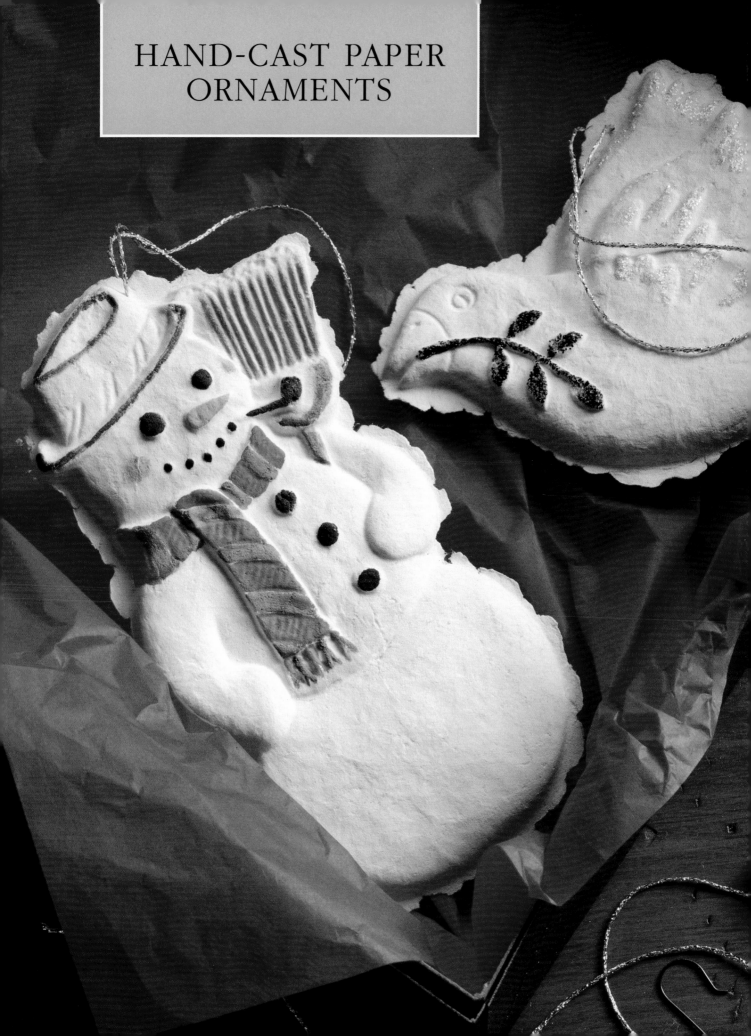

HAND-CAST PAPER
ORNAMENTS

Though they may appear to be very delicate, these hand-cast paper ornaments are durable enough to become lasting keepsakes. Cotton linter is soaked in water and processed to a pulp, using a household blender. Paper-casting powder is added to the pulp for strength. Water is then strained from the mixture, and the pulp is pressed into a ceramic mold and allowed to dry.

After the ornament is removed from the mold, it may be painted, using water-color paints, or shaded, using chalk pastels. Tiny sprigs of dried floral material and narrow ribbons may be added for a Victorian look. For sparkle, fine glitter may be applied.

Supplies for making hand-cast paper ornaments are available at craft or art supply stores. They may be purchased separately or in kit form. One sheet of cotton linter measuring 8" × 7" (20.5 × 18 cm) will produce enough pulp for three hand-cast paper ornaments. The decorative ceramic molds have many other uses, making them a worthwhile purchase. Preparation of the mold before casting may vary with each brand; read manufacturer's instructions before beginning the project.

Leftover pulp can be saved for later use. Squeeze out excess water, and spread the pulp out in small clumps to dry. It is not necessary to add more paper-casting powder when resoaking and processing leftover pulp.

MATERIALS

- Cotton linter.
- Paper-casting powder, such as paper clay or paper additive.
- Household blender.
- Strainer.
- Ceramic casting mold.
- Sponge.
- Kitchen towel.
- Narrow ribbon or cord, for hanger; darning needle, for inserting hanger.
- Watercolor paints or chalk pastels, optional.
- Embellishments, such as dried floral materials, narrow ribbons, and glitter, optional.
- Craft glue, or hot glue gun and glue sticks, optional.

HOW TO MAKE A HAND-CAST PAPER ORNAMENT

1 Tear 8" × 7" (20.5 × 18 cm) sheet of cotton linter into 1" (2.5 cm) pieces. Put in the blender with 1 quart (1 L) water; allow to soak for several minutes.

2 Blend the water and linter for 30 seconds on low speed. Add 1 teaspoon (5 mL) of paper-casting powder to mixture; blend on high speed for one minute.

3 Pour about one-third of mixture into strainer, draining off water. Put wet pulp into mold.

4 Spread pulp evenly around mold and out onto flat outer edges; pulp on flat edges will form deckled edge around border of ornament.

5 Press damp sponge over pulp, compressing it into the mold and drawing off excess water; wring out sponge. Repeat two or three times until excess water is removed.

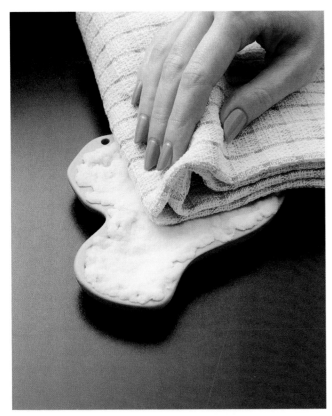

6 Press a folded kitchen towel over the compressed pulp, absorbing any remaining water and further compressing pulp.

7 Allow compressed pulp to dry completely in the mold. To speed drying, place the mold in an oven heated to 150°F (65°C) for about three hours.

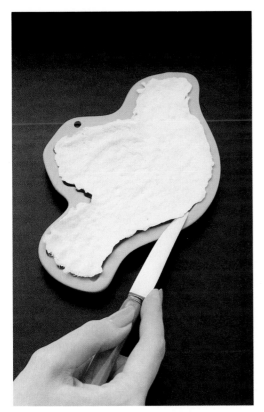

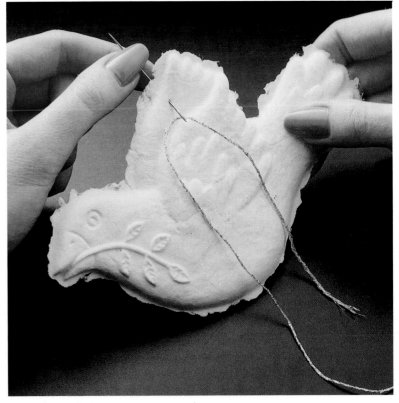

8 Loosen deckled edge of border around hand-cast paper ornament, using blade of knife; gently remove ornament from mold.

9 Thread cord or narrow ribbon into darning needle. Insert the needle through top of ornament at inner edge of border; knot ends of cord. Embellish ornament as desired (page 24).

TIPS FOR EMBELLISHING HAND-CAST PAPER ORNAMENTS

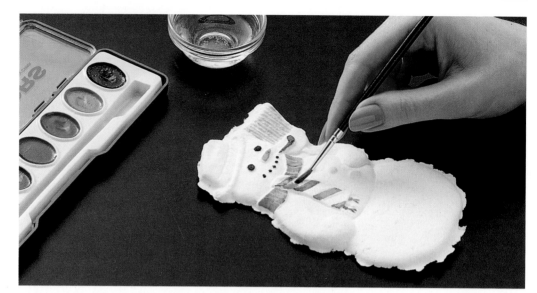

Painted ornaments.
Paint hand-cast paper
ornaments, using
diluted watercolors
and small brush.
Allow a painted area
to dry before painting
the adjacent area.

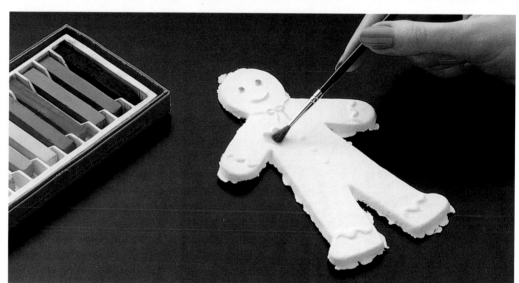

**Color-shaded
ornaments.** Shade
hand-cast paper orna-
ments, using chalk
pastels or cosmetic
powders. Apply with
small brush or small
foam applicator.

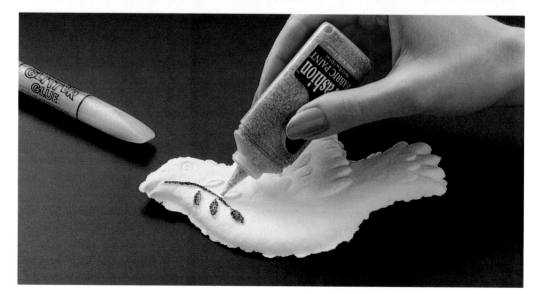

Glittered ornaments.
Outline or fill in small
areas, using glitter glue
in fine-tip tubes. Or,
for large areas, apply
glue over areas, using
glue pen or glue stick.
Sprinkle with glitter;
shake off excess.

LACE DOILY ORNAMENTS

Lace doily ornaments, shaped as wreaths, semicircles, and baskets, give a Victorian look to a Christmas tree.

By using the ornaments, instead of bows, on packages, they become an extra keepsake gift.

Make the ornaments easily from Battenberg lace or cutwork doilies. Add ribbon hangers, and embellish the ornaments with trimmings such as dried or silk flowers or pearl strands.

MATERIALS (for lace doily wreath or semicircle ornament)

- Two 6" (15 cm) Battenberg or cutwork doilies, for lace wreath, or one for lace semicircle.
- Polyester fiberfill.
- 9" (23 cm) length of ribbon or braid trim, for hanger.
- Embellishments, such as dried or silk floral materials, pearl strands, and ribbon.
- Hot glue gun and glue sticks, optional.

MATERIALS (for lace doily basket ornament)

- One 8" (20.5 cm) Battenberg or cutwork doily: one doily makes two ornaments.
- 9" (23 cm) length of ribbon or braid trim, for hanger.
- Embellishments, such as dried or silk floral materials, optional.
- Hot glue gun and glue sticks, optional.

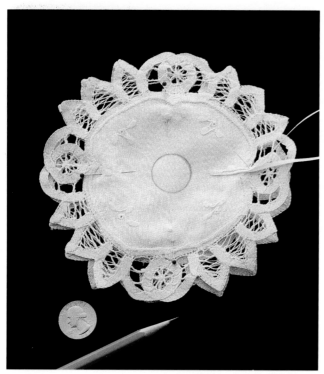

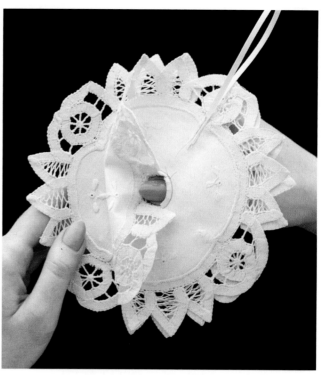

1 Baste ends of ribbon to wrong side of doily, about 1¼" (3.2 cm) from center. Mark 1" (2.5 cm) circle in center of one doily on wrong side. Pin the doilies right sides together.

2 Stitch around circle on marked line, using short stitch length. Trim away the fabric on the inside of circle ⅛" (3 mm) from stitching; turn right side out through center.

3 Stitch around the doilies, along the inner edge of lace trim, or 1" (2.5 cm) from the previous stitching; leave 2" (5 cm) opening.

4 Stuff the wreath with polyester fiberfill; stitch the opening closed by machine, using zipper foot. Secure embellishments with hot glue or by hand-stitching them in place.

HOW TO SEW A LACE DOILY SEMICIRCLE ORNAMENT

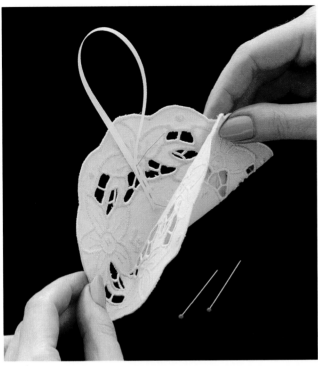

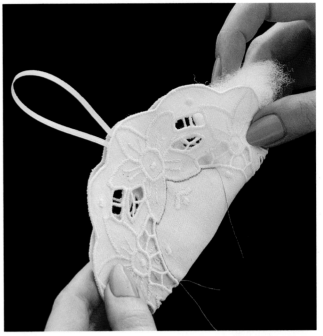

1 Baste ends of ribbon to wrong side of doily, about ¾" (2 cm) from center of doily. Fold doily in half.

2 Stitch around the semicircle, along inner edge of lace, or 1" (2.5 cm) from outer edge, using a short stitch length; leave 1" (2.5 cm) opening. Complete as in step 4, opposite.

HOW TO SEW A LACE DOILY BASKET ORNAMENT

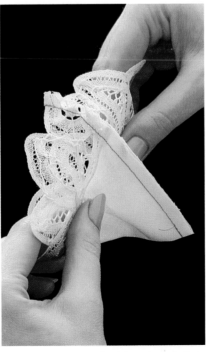

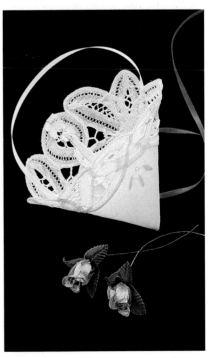

1 Cut doily in half. Fold one doily piece in half again, right sides together; mark point on raw edge at fold. Mark point on outer curved edge ½" (1.3 cm) from cut edge; draw line connecting points.

2 Cut on the marked line. Stitch ¼" (6 mm) from the raw edge, using short stitch length. Turn right side out; press.

3 Stitch ribbon to each side of the basket; seam is at the center back. Secure any embellishments with hot glue or by hand-stitching in place.

FELT ORNAMENTS

These finely detailed ornaments are fun and easy to make, using craft felt or synthetic suede. Choose from a traditional dove or reindeer, or a whimsical cat and mouse. The body of each ornament is stitched before it is cut, making for quick assembly. Polyester stuffing gives added dimension.

HOW TO MAKE A MOUSE ORNAMENT

MATERIALS

- Felt.
- Polyester fiberfill.
- Thick craft glue.
- Black fine-point permanent-ink marker.
- Scrap of fabric for shawl.
- Gray embroidery floss.

- Scrap of yellow cellulose sponge, about 3⁄8" (1 cm) thick, for cheese.
- 9" (23 cm) length of ribbon, 1⁄8" (3 mm) wide, for bow on cheese.
- 8" (20.5 cm) length of fine brass wire, for glasses.

CUTTING DIRECTIONS

From felt, cut two ears and four arms, using patterns on page 122. Also cut one 5" (12.5 cm) strip of felt a scant 1⁄4" (6 mm) wide, for tail. From fabric, cut one shawl, using pattern on page 122. Transfer mouse body pattern on page 122 onto heavy paper or cardboard; body is cut on page 30, step 3.

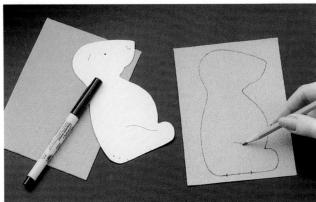

1 Place pattern for body on felt; using fine-point marker, trace around pattern. Lightly mark stitching line for leg definition, using pencil or chalk. Pin-mark tail placement. Place marked felt on second layer of felt.

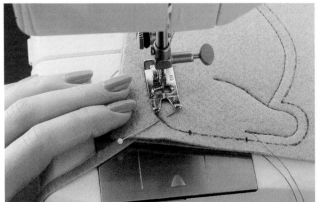

2 Stitch around body ¼" (6 mm) inside marked line and on markings for leg definition, inserting tail as indicated on pattern; leave opening for stuffing at lower edge of body.

(Continued)

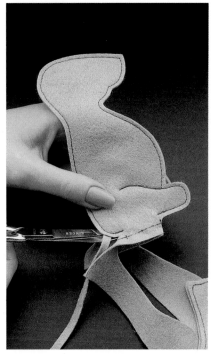

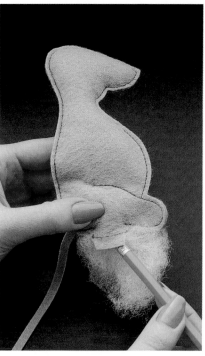

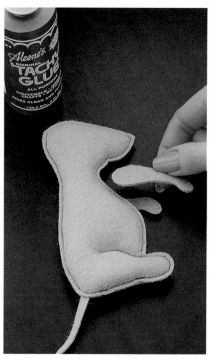

3 Trim felt ⅛" (3 mm) from the stitching, taking care not to trim off tail; do not trim at opening for stuffing.

4 Stuff body with polyester fiberfill. Stitch the opening closed, using zipper foot; trim felt ⅛" (3 mm) from stitching.

5 Glue two arm pieces together, matching edges; repeat for remaining arm. Allow glue to dry. Glue one arm to each side of body, as indicated on pattern. Allow glue to dry.

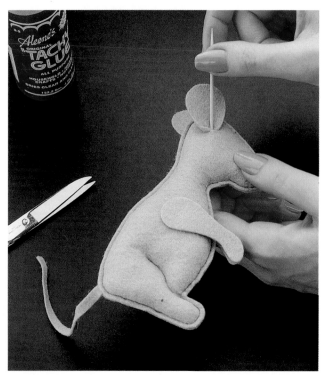

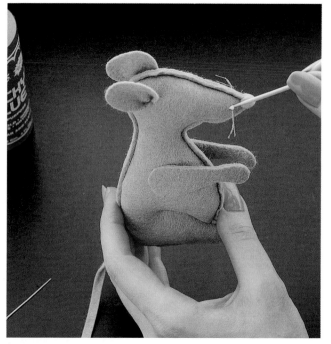

6 Cut slit for ear, about ¼" (6 mm) long, as indicated on pattern. Insert lower edge of ear into opening, using a toothpick. Secure the ear with small dot of glue. Repeat for remaining ear.

7 Cut two ¼" (6 mm) circles from pink felt; glue to each side of the snout as shown. Thread needle with three strands of gray embroidery floss, and insert through nose for whiskers; trim to ¾" (2 cm) on each side of nose. Using toothpick, place small dot of glue at the base of whiskers to secure.

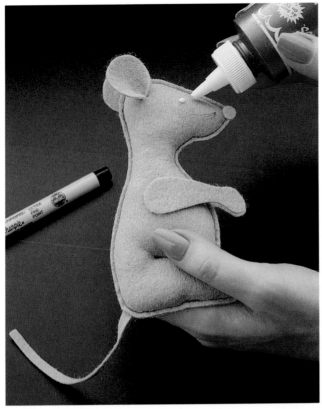

8 Apply small dot of fabric glue to felt at eye marks, as indicated on pattern. When glue is dry, mark each eye, using black permanent-ink marker.

9 Form glasses by wrapping wire around a pen to make the first lens opening; twist wire to secure. Repeat to make the second lens, spacing circles about ½" (1.3 cm) apart. Place glasses on nose; secure by wrapping ends of wire around ears. Trim excess wire.

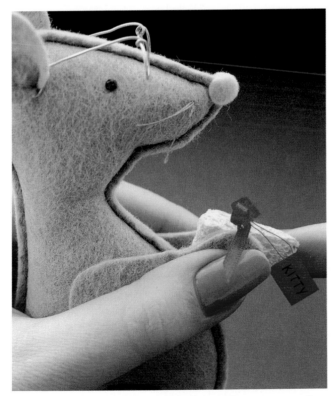

10 Cut wedge about 1" (2.5 cm) long from sponge, for cheese. Tie ribbon bow around cheese. Make gift tag from scrap of colored paper; secure to ribbon bow, using thread. Glue cheese to front paws.

11 Tie shawl around neck of the mouse. Secure loop of embroidery floss through top of the ornament, for hanger.

HOW TO MAKE A CAT ORNAMENT

MATERIALS

- Felt.
- Polyester fiberfill.
- Thick craft glue.
- Black fine-point permanent-ink marker.
- Miniature novelty mouse.
- 9" (23 cm) length of ribbon, 1/8" (3 mm) wide, for bow at neck.
- Brown embroidery floss, for whiskers.
- Pipe cleaner.

CUTTING DIRECTIONS

Cut two ears and one muzzle, using patterns on page 122. Cut two 1¼" × 5" (3.2 × 12.5 cm) rectangles, for tail. Transfer body and hindquarters patterns on page 122 onto heavy paper or cardboard; these pieces are cut below.

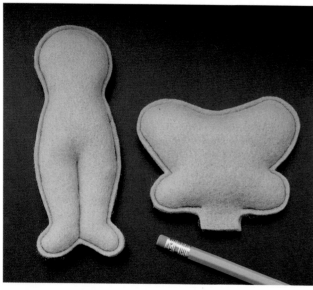

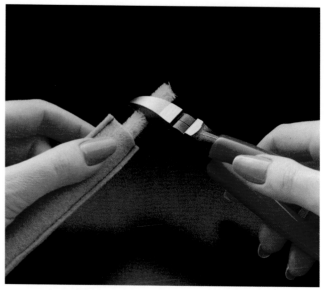

1 Assemble front body section as for mouse on pages 29 and 30, steps 1 to 4, omitting reference to tail; in step 2, leave opening just below neck, for stuffing. Repeat to make hindquarters section, leaving opening at lower edge, for stuffing and tail placement; do not stitch hindquarters section closed.

2 Layer tail pieces. Stitch around tail, using ¼" (6 mm) seam allowance and rounding corners at one end; leave opposite end open. Trim felt 1/8" (3 mm) from stitching. Insert pipe cleaner into tail; trim pipe cleaner ½" (1.3 cm) from edge of felt.

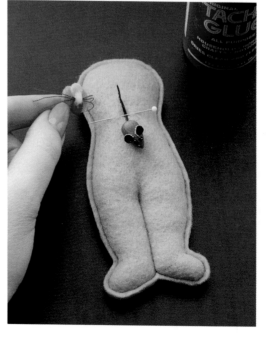

3 Insert the tail into hindquarters section; complete stitching. Trim the excess felt, taking care not to cut tail.

4 Cut one scant ¼" (6 mm) circle each from pink and red felt; glue to wrong side of muzzle piece as shown. Glue three 2" (5 cm) strands of brown embroidery floss to wrong side of muzzle, for whiskers. Glue muzzle unit to face, as indicated on pattern, tucking tail of novelty mouse under the muzzle.

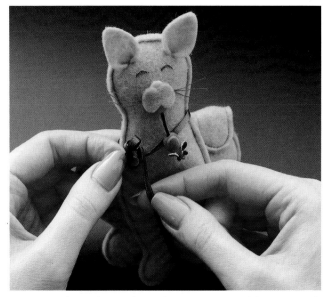

5 Attach the ears as on page 30, step 6. Mark the eyes as on page 31, step 8. Hand-stitch or glue the body to the hindquarters.

6 Shape the tail into desired position. Tie ribbon around the neck. Secure loop of embroidery floss through top of ornament, for hanger.

HOW TO MAKE A REINDEER ORNAMENT

MATERIALS

- Felt.
- Polyester fiberfill; pipe cleaner.
- Thick craft glue; embroidery floss.
- Black fine-point permanent-ink marker.
- Golf tee, for horn; craft acrylic glitter paint.

CUTTING DIRECTIONS

From felt, cut two ears, two antlers, and one tail, using patterns on page 123. Cut one ½" × 8" (1.3 × 20.5 cm) rectangle for the scarf. Transfer body and leg patterns on page 123 onto heavy paper or cardboard; these pieces are cut below.

1 Glue antler pieces together, matching edges. Fold tail in half lengthwise; pin. Assemble reindeer leg section as for the mouse body on pages 29 and 30, steps 1 to 3, omitting reference to tail. Insert pipe cleaner into leg; trim pipe cleaner ¼" (1.3 cm) from edge of felt.

2 Repeat step 1 on page 29 to prepare reindeer body section for stitching; pin-mark placement for antlers, tail, and extended leg. Stitch around body, inserting the antlers, tail, and leg at markings; leave opening at upper edge of back for stuffing.

(Continued)

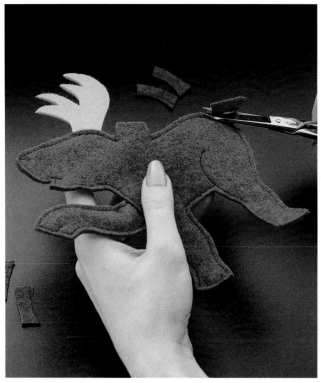

3 Trim felt ⅛" (3 mm) from stitching, taking care not to cut antlers, tail, or front leg. Stuff body with polyester fiberfill. Stitch opening closed, using zipper foot.

4 Attach ears as on page 30, step 6. Mark eyes as on page 31, step 8.

5 Apply glitter paint to golf tee; allow to dry. Glue golf tee to leg as shown, for horn.

6 Cut slits at ends of scarf piece to make fringe, using scissors. Tie scarf around neck of reindeer. Secure loop of embroidery floss through top of ornament, for hanger.

HOW TO MAKE A DOVE ORNAMENT

MATERIALS

- Felt.
- Polyester fiberfill.
- Thick craft glue; embroidery floss.
- Black fine-point permanent-ink marker.
- Small artificial leaves.

CUTTING DIRECTIONS

Transfer body and wing patterns on page 123 onto heavy paper or cardboard; these pieces are cut below.

1 Assemble body section as for mouse on pages 29 and 30, steps 1 to 4, omitting reference to tail. Repeat to make two wings, omitting stuffing.

2 Glue a wing to each side of the body, staggering the placement slightly so both the wings are visible from each side.

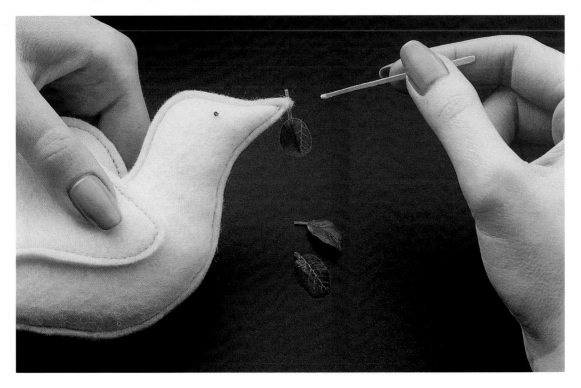

3 Mark eyes as on page 31, step 8. Glue artificial leaves to beak. Secure a loop of embroidery floss through the top of ornament, for the hanger.

RIBBON ROSES

Ribbon roses add an elegant touch to the Christmas tree. They are constructed using either standard ribbon for a traditional rose or wired ribbon for a cabbage-style rose, and are secured to wire stems. The stems are wrapped with floral tape, with artificial leaves inserted for a finishing touch.

Make roses of different sizes, using ribbon in different widths. The length of the ribbon needed for each rose varies with the width of the ribbon and the desired finished size. A rose made with ⅝" (1.5 cm) ribbon may require ½ yd. (0.5 m) of ribbon, while a rose made with 2¼" (6 cm) ribbon may require 1½ yd. (1.4 m) of ribbon. For impact, cluster several roses of different colors and sizes, forming a ribbon rose bouquet. Simply twist the wire stems of the roses around the tree branches to secure them to the tree.

MATERIALS

- Medium-gauge stem wire.
- Fine-gauge paddle floral wire, for traditional ribbon roses.
- Ribbon in desired width, for traditional rose, or wired ribbon in desired width, for cabbage-style rose; width of ribbon and desired finished size of rose determine length needed.
- Artificial rose leaves.
- Floral tape.

HOW TO MAKE A TRADITIONAL RIBBON ROSE

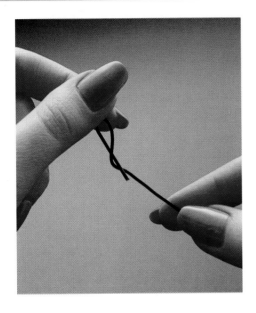

1 Bend a 1" (2.5 cm) loop in the end of stem wire; twist to secure.

2 Fold ribbon end over loop; wrap with paddle floral wire to secure.

(Continued)

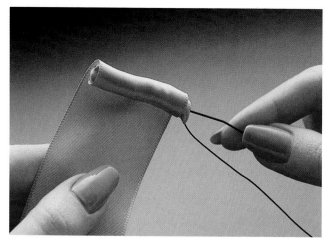

3 Hold ribbon taut in left hand and stem wire in right hand; roll stem wire toward left hand, wrapping ribbon tightly around the fold three times, forming rose center. Wrap paddle wire tightly around base to secure.

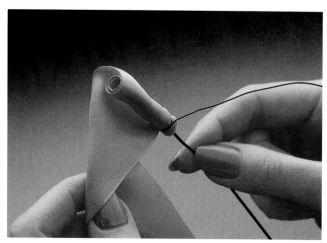

4 Fold ribbon back diagonally as shown, close to rose. Roll rose center over fold, keeping upper edge of rose center just below upper edge of fold; lower edges of ribbon will not be aligned.

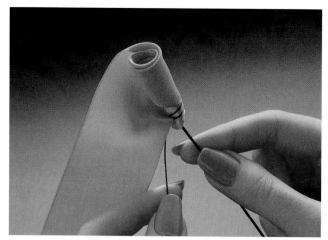

5 Roll to end of fold, forming petal. Wrap paddle wire tightly around base.

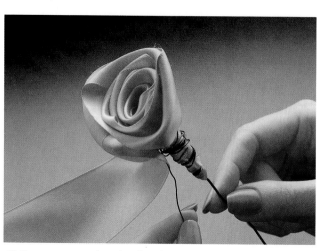

6 Repeat steps 4 and 5 for desired number of petals. Fold ribbon back diagonally, and secure with paddle wire at base; cut ribbon and paddle wire.

7 Wrap end of floral tape around base of rose, stretching tape slightly for best adhesion. Wrap entire base of rose, concealing wire. Continue wrapping floral tape onto stem wire. Place stem of artificial rose leaf next to stem wire; wrap stem wire and leaf stem together with floral tape. Continue wrapping until entire stem wire is covered with floral tape.

HOW TO MAKE A CABBAGE-STYLE ROSE

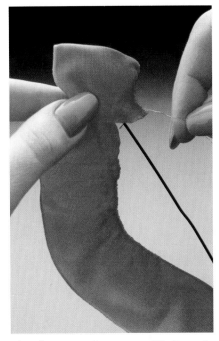

1 Follow step 1 on page 37. Cut a 1 to 1½-yd. (0.95 to 1.4 m) length of wired ribbon. Pull out about 2" (5 cm) of wire on one edge of one end of ribbon. Fold ribbon end over loop; secure with pulled wire, forming rose center.

2 Gather up one edge of remaining length of ribbon tightly by sliding ribbon along ribbon wire toward the rose center.

3 Wrap the gathered edge around the base of the rose, wrapping each layer slightly higher than the previous layer.

4 Fold the ribbon end down and catch under last layer. Wrap ribbon wire tightly around base several times to secure. Cut off excess ribbon wire.

5 Follow step 7, opposite, covering gathered edge of ribbon and wire.

MORE
IDEAS FOR
ORNAMENTS

Nature elements *are used to embellish a miniature basket and wreath, creating clever ornaments. Miniature basket ornament is filled with sprigs of greenery and artificial berries. Miniature wreath is embellished with a small craft bird, sprigs of greenery, and artificial berries.*

Ribbon, lace, and small cones
(right) turn a plain ornament into
an elegant tree decoration. Secure
the embellishments using dots of
clear-drying glue.

Torn fabric strips are tied
around a cinnamon stick to make
a Christmas tree ornament (below).
Whole allspice and anise are used
for embellishment. Secure raffia
hanger with hot glue.

Large cones, painted like Santas,
(below) make quick and inexpensive
ornaments. Secure strings for the
hangers, using a drop of hot glue.
Form the face, beard, and hairline,
using artificial snow paste; then
paint the ornament, using acrylic
paints. Trim the top of the completed
ornament with snow paste.

QUICK & EASY GARLANDS

Candy canes and mint candies are tied together with red ribbon for a colorful garland.

Large bells embellished with cones and sprigs of greenery are tied together with raffia.

Holiday garlands are traditionally used to decorate the Christmas tree. Make your own garlands by securing items such as candies, cookie cutters, or floral materials together with ribbon, raffia, or fabric strips.

Mini cookie cutters *in Christmas shapes are strung on lengths of jute. Beads are interspersed between the cookie cutters to add color to the garland.*

Pretzels, *tied to torn strips of fabric, make a country-style garland.*

LAYERED TREE SKIRTS

Decorate the base of a Christmas tree with a layered tree skirt embellished with ribbon bows. When arranged around the tree, it resembles an eight-pointed star. The skirt can be made for either an elegant or casual look, depending on the choice of fabrics and ribbon.

Easy to make, the tree skirt is simply two lined squares of fabric, stitched together around center openings. Back openings in the layers allow for easy placement around the tree. Safety pins, used in place of permanent stitching, gather the fabric along each side, saving time and allowing the tree skirt to be stored flat.

Choose a lightweight lining fabric to prevent adding bulk to the skirt. For an inexpensive lining that is also a good choice for sheer fabrics, use nylon net.

Layered tree skirt *is made from printed and plaid complementary holiday fabrics. Solid-colored fabrics are used for the lining. The tree skirt is embellished with wired ribbon bows.*

MATERIALS

- 1¼ yd. (1.15 m) each, of two coordinating fabrics.
- 1¼ yd. (1.15 m) each, of two lining fabrics.
- Eight large safety pins.
- Wired ribbon.

HOW TO MAKE A LAYERED TREE SKIRT

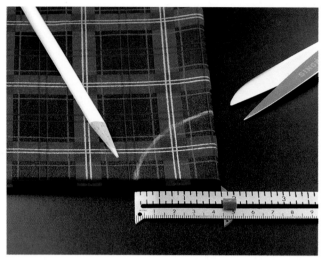

1 Cut outer fabric into a square, trimming selvages. Fold fabric in half lengthwise, then crosswise. Mark an arc, measuring 1¾" (4.5 cm) from folded center of fabric. Cut on marked line.

2 Pin-mark one folded edge at raw edges for the center back opening; open fabric and mark cutting line from raw edge to center opening, on wrong side of fabric.

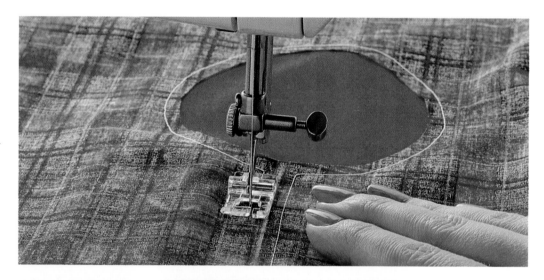

3 Place face fabric on lining, right sides together; pin the layers together. Stitch ¼" (6 mm) seam around tree skirt, stitching around all edges and on each side of center back line; leave 6" (15 cm) opening for turning. For sheer fabrics, stitch a second row scant ⅛" (3 mm) from first stitching.

4 Cut on marked line; trim lining even with edges of outer fabric. Clip seam allowances around center circle; trim corners diagonally. Turn right side out; press. Slipstitch opening closed.

5 Repeat steps 1 to 4 for the remaining tree skirt layer. Align skirts, right sides up, matching center back openings. Shift the upper skirt so corners of the lower skirt are centered at sides of upper skirt. Mark opening of lower skirt on upper skirt. Pin layers together around the center from marked point to opening in the upper skirt.

6 Topstitch ¼" (6 mm) from the raw edges around center, from opening to marked point, securing the two tree skirt layers together.

7 Gather and bunch fabric at the center of one long edge by inserting point of safety pin in and out of fabric for about 6" (15 cm) on lining side of the tree skirt as shown; close the pin. Repeat at center of each side for each tree skirt layer; do not pin back opening sides.

8 Place skirt around base of tree. Overlap back opening at outer edge; gather and bunch fabric for underlayer with safety pin. Repeat for remaining center back opening of upper layer of skirt.

9 Make four ribbon bows. Position a bow at each side of the upper layer, concealing safety pin; secure with pin.

MORE
IDEAS FOR
TREE
SKIRTS

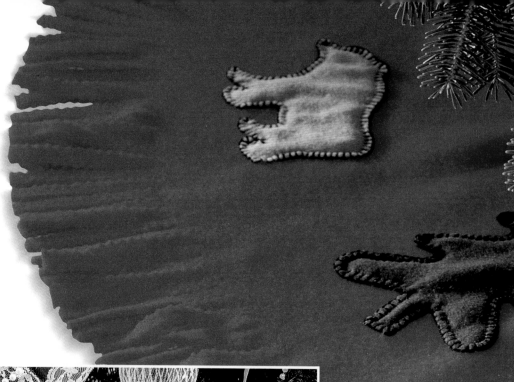

**Polar
fleece tree
skirt** *(above),
with fringed edges,
requires no sewing.
To make the round
skirt, mark an arc for
the outside of the circle
and cut as on page 112,
step 2. Mark the arc for
the center opening, and
cut as on page 46, step 1.
Apply the appliqués as
for the fleece throw
(page 71). Cut the fringe,
keeping the blade of the
scissors perpendicular to
the edge of the fabric.*

Lace tablecloth,
*draped around the
base of a tree,
complements a
Victorian-style tree.*

Excelsior, *highlighted with gold spray paint, is arranged around the base of a Christmas tree for a unique accent.*

SHINGLED TREES

Make a grouping of woodland trees in various sizes to accent a holiday table or to display on a mantel. The trees are made using Styrofoam® cones and miniature wooden shingles. For additional color and texture, the trees can be trimmed with wooden cutouts, such as stars, birds, or snowflakes. Or embellish them with miniature beaded garlands.

MATERIALS

- Styrofoam cone, with height of 6" (15 cm), 9" (23 cm), or 12" (30.5 cm), depending on desired tree size.
- Miniature wooden shingles.
- Green paper twist.
- Green acrylic paint; soft-bristled paintbrush.
- Hot glue gun and glue sticks.
- Embellishments, such as miniature wooden cutouts or beaded garland.

HOW TO MAKE A SHINGLED TREE

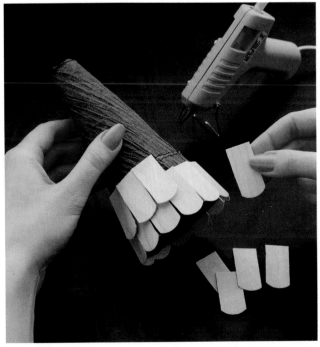

1 Glue paper twist around cone, piecing as necessary to cover Styrofoam. Cut a circle of paper twist to diameter of cone base; glue to bottom of cone.

2 Apply hot glue to lower edge of paper-wrapped cone, gluing about 4" (10 cm) at a time. Secure a row of shingles around cone, with the lower edge of the shingles extending about 3/8" (1 cm) below cone. Glue a second row, overlapping shingles about one-half the length of the shingle and staggering placement as shown.

(Continued)

3 Continue applying rows of shingles, overlapping upper edges of shingles at sides as necessary. At upper portion of tree, clip corners of shingles as necessary.

4 Trim four shingles to a point at upper edge as shown, using utility scissors. Glue trimmed shingles to top of cone to complete tree.

5 Dilute green acrylic paint with water. Apply thinned paint liberally to tree, taking care to apply paint to underside of shingles where underside is visible.

6 Embellish tree as desired with wooden cutouts or beaded garland.

TIERED
WOOD
TREES

An easy woodworking project, the tiered wood Christmas tree is made by stacking graduated lengths of screen molding on a wooden dowel. The branches of the tree are movable, allowing for ease in storage. Supplies for the tiered tree can be purchased at craft or lumber supply stores. Finished trees can be decorated with miniature ornaments or garlands, if desired. Unadorned trees are suitable for seasonal decorating all winter.

MATERIALS

- Three 8' (244 cm) lengths screen molding.
- Jigsaw, drill and ¼" drill bit.
- Fine-grit sandpaper; file.
- ¼" (6 mm) wooden dowel.
- Wooden block, 1½" (3.8 cm) square.
- Wooden ball knob, 1¼" (3.2 cm) in diameter.
- Wooden base in desired shape, 5" to 7" (12.5 to 18 cm) wide.
- Wood stain; soft cloth.
- Wood glue.
- Miniature ornaments or garlands, optional.

CUTTING DIRECTIONS

Cut each 8' (244 cm) length of screen molding into eight 12" (30.5 cm) pieces. Reserve three 12" 30.5 cm) pieces for the lower branches. Cut off and discard 1" (2.5 cm) from three pieces, to make three 11" (28 cm) branches.

Cut the remaining pieces into four branches each, of the following lengths: 10" (25.5 cm), 9" (23 cm), 8" (20.5 cm), 7" (18 cm), 6" (15 cm), 5" (12.5 cm), 4" (10 cm), 3" (7.5 cm), and 2" (5 cm).

HOW TO MAKE A TIERED WOOD TREE

1 Drill hole through center of each branch, using ¼" drill bit. Sand all surfaces of the branches, using fine-grit sandpaper; use file to smooth the rough edges around hole.

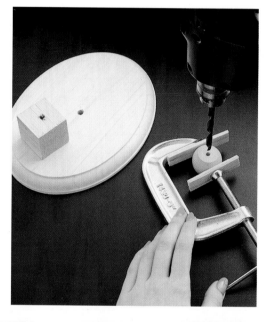

2 Drill hole through the center of wooden block, using ¼" drill bit; repeat for wooden base. Enlarge hole in wooden ball knob, using ¼" drill bit and drilling about ⅜" (1 cm) into ball knob; hold the knob securely in the clamp, using scraps of wood to protect sides. Sand the wooden block, base, and ball knob, using sandpaper.

3 Stain all pieces of tree with wood stain, applying stain with soft cloth, following manufacturer's directions. Allow to dry.

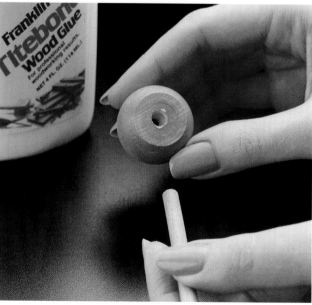

4 Apply wood glue to hole in ball knob; insert the end of ¼" (6 mm) wooden dowel into hole.

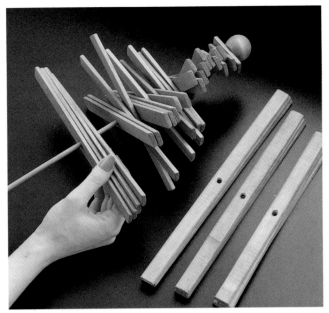

5 Slide tree branches onto dowel, beginning with 2" (5 cm) branches and continuing in order, according to size; keep rounded side of branches facing toward top of tree.

6 Slide wooden block onto dowel; slide wooden base onto dowel. Check to see that all pieces stack snugly together; mark dowel where it exits bottom of base.

7 Remove base; cut dowel at mark.

9 Spread branches of tree in pleasing arrangement. Decorate with miniature ornaments or garlands, if desired.

8 Apply wood glue to the bottom of wooden block and around end of wooden dowel. Insert dowel into hole in base; position block as desired. Allow glue to dry.

CAROLERS

Pose a pair of carolers, complete with a lamppost, on a table or mantel to spread holiday cheer. Crafted using wooden dowels and ball knobs, each piece is easy to assemble. The garments are assembled using simple rectangular fabric pieces, requiring no patterns and minimal sewing.

The carolers can be made in a variety of styles, depending on the fabrics chosen. For a country look, select fabrics such as corduroy or flannel. For a more elegant look, use fabrics such as velvet or taffeta. Floral wire in each arm allows the figures to be posed, holding a variety of embellishments.

MATERIALS (for pair of carolers and lamppost)

- Three wooden plaques, for base of each piece.
- Two 2" (5 cm) wooden balls, for heads.
- Four 1" (2.5 cm) wooden ball knobs, for feet.
- One 2¼" (6 cm) wooden ball knob, for lamppost.
- Four 18 mm wooden beads, for hands.
- Four 8" (20.5 cm) lengths of ⅝" (1.5 cm) dowel, for legs.
- One 11" (28 cm) length of ¾" (2 cm) dowel, for lamppost.
- Drill; ¹⁄₁₆" and ⅛" drill bits.
- Six 6 × 1⅝" (4 cm) drywall screws.
- One ³⁄₁₆ × 2" (5 cm) dowel screw; four 19 × ½" (1.3 cm) wire nails.
- 22-gauge paddle floral wire.
- Fabric scraps, for pants, shirt, and dress.

- Buttons, for shirt.
- Scrap of Ultrasuede® or felt, for cap.
- Scrap of ribbing, for leggings.
- ½ yd. (0.5 m) trim, such as gimp trim or ribbon, for pants.
- ⅝ yd. (0.6 m) eyelet or lace, at least 6" (15 cm) wide, for slip.
- ⅜ yd. (0.35 m) eyelet or lace, about 1" (2.5 cm) wide, for neck trim of dress.
- ¼" (6 mm) pom-pom, for cap.
- Doll hair; polyester fiberfill.
- Craft glue; adhesive felt.
- Acrylic gloss enamel paints; artist's brushes.
- Embellishments, such as miniature evergreen garland, ribbon, and small cones, for lamppost.

CUTTING DIRECTIONS

For the boy caroler, cut two 5½" (14 cm) squares from the fabric for the pants. For the shirt, cut one 4" × 12" (10 × 30.5 cm) rectangle for the body of the shirt and two 5" × 6" (12.5 × 15 cm) rectangles for the sleeves. For the scarf, cut one 1" × 14" (2.5 × 35.5 cm) rectangle. For the cap, cut one 1½" (3.8 cm) circle and one 4" (10 cm) circle from felt or Ultrasuede; cut the smaller circle in half for the brim.

For the girl caroler, cut one 6" × 20" (15 × 51 cm) rectangle for the slip. For the dress, cut one 12" × 20" (30.5 × 51 cm) rectangle. Cut two 5" × 6" (12.5 × 15 cm) rectangles for the sleeves of the dress. For the leggings, cut two 3" × 4" (7.5 × 10 cm) rectangles from ribbing, placing the rib of the fabric on the longest edge.

HOW TO MAKE A BOY CAROLER

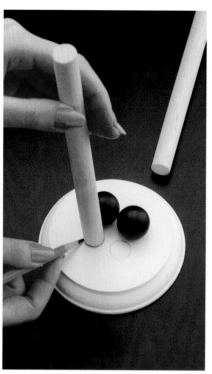

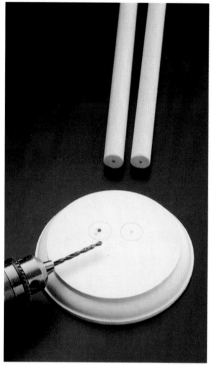

1 Paint 1" (2.5 cm) ball knobs for feet as desired. Paint 2" (5 cm) ball knob for head and 18 mm beads for hands flesh color. Paint or stain base plaque as desired.

2 Position dowels and ball knobs for feet on the plaque for desired placement, with dowels 1/4" (6 mm) apart. Mark the position for dowels, using a pencil as shown.

3 Mark placement for screw in the center of each marking for dowel; mark center of each dowel at one end. Predrill holes at marks, using 1/8" drill bit.

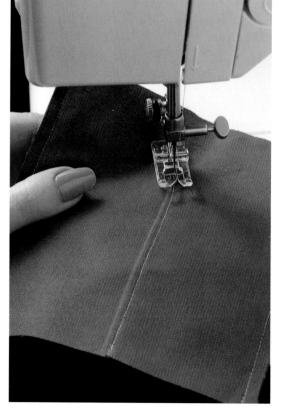

4 Secure dowels to base plaque, inserting screws from bottom of plaque.

5 Mark a 4" (10 cm) line, centered as shown, on wrong side of one pants piece, for pants inseam. Place pants pieces right sides together. Stitch 1/4" (6 mm) side seams. Stitch inseam, stitching 1/8" (3 mm) from marked line and tapering stitches to line at top. With the needle down, rotate fabric and repeat stitching on remaining side of marked line.

6 Cut inseam on marked line; press seam allowances on sides open. Turn pants right side out. Using hand running stitches and double-threaded needle, stitch close to upper edge of pants, leaving thread tails. Repeat at lower edge of each pants leg.

7 Fold rectangle for body of shirt, wrong sides together, matching the short edges; stitch ½" (1.3 cm) from the folded edge to make center tuck.

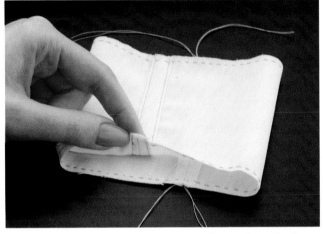

8 Press tuck, centering over seam; edgestitch on both sides through all layers. Fold the rectangle right sides together, matching short edges; stitch ¼" (6 mm) seam. Press seam allowances open, and turn tube right side out. Using hand running stitches and double-threaded needle, stitch close to upper edge of shirt, leaving thread tails. Repeat at lower edge.

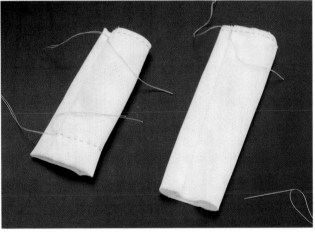

9 Fold rectangle for sleeve, right sides together, matching long edges; stitch ¼" (6 mm) seam. Press seam allowances open; turn tube right side out. Stitch row of hand running stitches close to upper edge. Fold under 1" (2.5 cm) at lower edge; stitch row of running stitches ¾" (2 cm) from folded edge. Repeat for other sleeve.

10 Slip pants over the dowels, inserting one dowel in each leg of pants. Gather lower edge of each leg, and knot thread. Slip shirt over dowels; gather and knot lower edge of shirt, centering tuck and back seam. Glue lower edge of shirt to dowels; allow upper edge of shirt to extend slightly above top of the dowels.

11 Gather and knot upper edge of the pants; secure with glue. Secure gimp at waist and ankles. Glue feet to base. Lightly stuff body of the shirt with polyester fiberfill as necessary. Gather and knot the upper edge of the shirt; glue to dowels. Glue buttons to shirt.

(Continued)

12 Cut wire about 16" (40.5 cm) in length. Secure the wire to the ends of dowels by wrapping wire around a wire nail inserted into each dowel; to prevent splitting the wood, predrill, using 1/16" drill bit.

13 Thread bead onto wire; wrap end of wire as shown so length of arm is about 3½" (9 cm). Repeat for opposite side.

14 Slip sleeve over wire arm. Gather and knot the upper edge of sleeve, centering seam down inside of arm; glue sleeve to upper edge of shirt. Lightly stuff the sleeve with polyester fiberfill. Tightly gather lower edge of sleeve; secure with knot. Repeat for second sleeve.

15 Glue head to top of dowels. Cut and glue individual lengths of doll hair to head for hair, working in sections; for the bangs, glue short pieces across front of head.

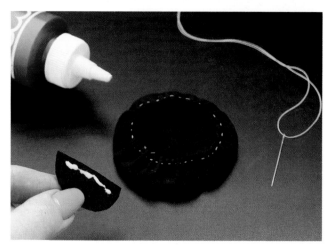

16 Stitch row of hand running stitches close to edge of 4" (10 cm) circle for beret. Gather circle to measure about 2¾" (7 cm) in diameter; knot the thread. Glue brim in place.

17 Stuff the cap lightly with polyester fiberfill. Glue the pom-pom to center of cap. Glue cap to caroler. Cut fringe on ends of scarf; tie scarf around neck.

18 Draw eyes and mouth as shown, using fine-point permanent-ink marker.

19 Place caroler on paper side of adhesive felt; trace around the base. Cut felt just inside the marked lines. Remove the paper backing, and secure felt to the bottom of the base. Secure any embellishments as desired.

HOW TO MAKE A GIRL CAROLER

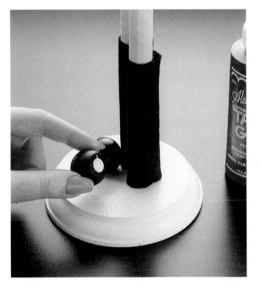

1 Follow page 60, steps 1 to 4. Fold rectangle for leggings right sides together, matching long edges; stitch ¼" (6 mm) seam. Turn tube right side out. Repeat for other legging. Slip one legging over each dowel leg, with seam centered down back of leg. Secure at lower edge with craft glue. Glue feet to base.

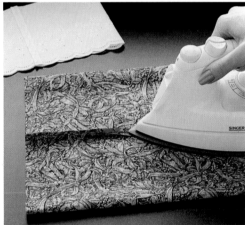

2 Fold the lace for slip right sides together, matching short ends; stitch ¼" (6 mm) seam. Press seam open. Repeat for dress.

3 Fold the dress lengthwise, with wrong sides together and raw edges even; lightly press folded edge. Pin-mark lower edge of the dress 2⅜" (6.2 cm) to each side of dress center front and center back.

(Continued)

4 Stitch from pin mark at edge of dress to 1½" (3.8 cm) from the edge, using double-threaded needle. Stitch back to edge of skirt ⅛" (3 mm) from previous stitching as shown; leave thread tails. Repeat at remaining pin marks.

5 Place slip, right side out, inside dress, with raw edges even. Using hand running stitches, stitch close to the upper raw edges, stitching through all layers and leaving thread tails.

6 Gather the lower edge of dress at stitching, to create scalloped edge; knot threads to secure. Glue or stitch ribbon rose at peak of each scallop.

7 Assemble sleeves as on page 61, step 9. Slip the dress over dowels. Tightly gather upper edge, and knot the thread; glue dress to dowels at upper edge.

8 Attach wire arms and sleeves as on page 62, steps 12 to 14.

9 Glue on head and hair as on page 62, step 15. Stitch hand running stitches in heading of lace for neck trim. Gather and glue the lace around the neck, positioning raw edges at back of caroler. Complete caroler, following page 63, steps 18 and 19.

HOW TO MAKE A LAMPPOST

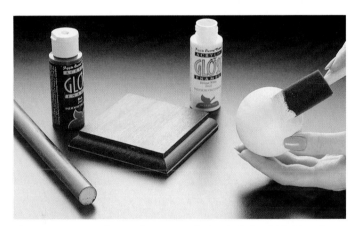

1 Paint or stain base plaque as desired. Paint ¾" (2 cm) dowel black for post. Paint 2¼" (6 cm) ball knob antique white for light globe.

2 Position the dowel as desired on base plaque; mark position, using pencil. Secure dowel to base as on page 60, steps 3 and 4. Predrill screw hole for dowel screw into upper end of dowel, using ⅛" drill bit; secure the dowel screw.

3 Secure the ball knob to dowel. Wrap the lamppost with garland, securing with hot glue. Embellish the light globe as desired. Attach felt to base as on page 63, step 19.

WOOLEN STOCKINGS

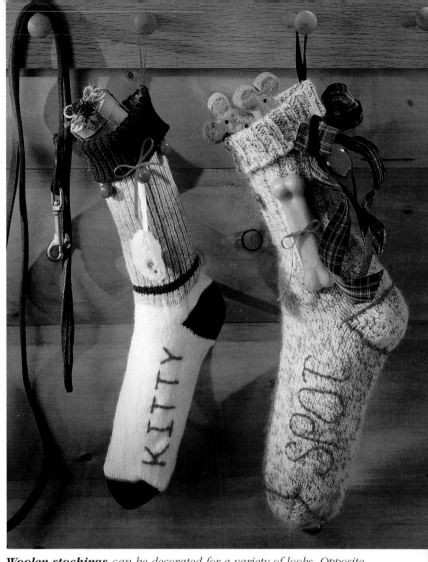

Turn woolen socks into personalized, one-of-a-kind Christmas stockings. Right at home hanging on a mantel, they also make a fun accent hung from an armoire.

Choose trims that complement the homespun look of the stockings. Add patches of flannel or wool fabric, and trims such as buttons, bells, or fringe. For a cuff, simply turn down the top of the sock. Or hand-stitch a fabric cuff to the top of the stocking. Most items can be stitched in place using a darning needle and narrow ribbon, yarn, or pearl cotton.

Wool socks are available at stores specializing in outdoor clothing. For extra-long stockings, purchase cross-country ski socks.

Woolen stockings *can be decorated for a variety of looks. Opposite, a stocking is embellished with sprigs of greenery and cones. Another features a snowman design, stitched in place using blanket stitches as on page 71. Above, stockings are custom-designed for family pets.*

TIPS FOR MAKING WOOLEN STOCKINGS

Insert a cardboard liner, cut slightly larger than the sock, into the sock before decorating with hand stitching; the liner will prevent catching stitches in the back of the sock.

Stitch letters, using yarn and back-stitches; secure stitches by taking one or two concealed small stitches.

Knot a loop of ribbon through top of sock for a hanger. Stuff finished stocking with tissue paper or with polyester fiberfill.

FLEECE THROWS

Synthetic fleece, such as Polartec®, is a warm, washable fabric that can be used to create a cozy holiday throw. The throw is appliquéd with simple Christmas motifs cut from scraps of fleece. The motifs can be appliquéd to the throw using either hand running stitches or blanket stitches. Because the fleece does not ravel, side hems are sewn with decorative hand stitches. Fringe is created along the upper and lower edges by making cuts with pinking shears.

MATERIALS

- 2 yd. (1.85 m) synthetic fleece, 60" (152.5 cm) wide, for throw.
- Synthetic fleece scraps in desired colors, for appliqués.
- Pinking shears.
- #3 pearl cotton; darning needle.

CUTTING DIRECTIONS

Cut off the selvages on the sides of the throw, using pinking shears. Cut simple Christmas motifs from scraps of fleece; use pinking shears for motifs that are to be appliquéd with running stitches, and use knife-edge shears for motifs that are to be appliquéd with blanket stitches.

HOW TO MAKE A FLEECE THROW

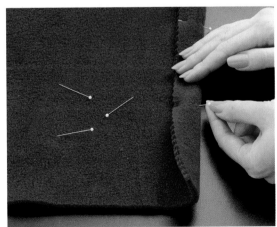

1 Fold 1" (2.5 cm) to wrong side along pinked edges, forming side hems; pin.

(Continued)

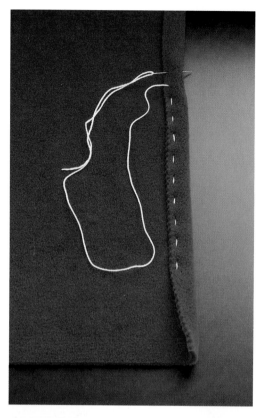

2 Stitch side hems ¼" (6 mm) from pinked edges, using #3 pearl cotton and darning needle; sew running stitch, beginning 4" (10 cm) from lower edge and ending 4" (10 cm) from upper edge, spacing stitches about ½" (1.3 cm) apart. Use stabbing motion, completing one stitch at a time, so stitches look the same on front and back.

3 Mark fabric at ½" (1.3 cm) intervals, 4" (10 cm) from lower raw edge, using water-soluble marking pen or chalk pencil; begin at inner edge of side hems.

4 Move ruler to raw edge; mark as in step 3. Cut slashes for fringe from outer marks to inner marks, using pinking shears. Cut slashes through the centers of hem allowances at sides. Mark and cut fringe at upper edge.

5 Arrange appliqués on front of throw as desired; pin. Stitch appliqués to throw, using #3 pearl cotton and darning needle; secure pinked appliqués using running stitches spaced about ¼" (6 mm) apart, or secure straight-cut appliqués using blanket stitch, opposite.

1 Knot end of single-strand pearl cotton; secure to the underside of appliqué, ¼" (6 mm) from outer edge. Form loop at edge of appliqué by bringing thread to left and then right as shown; hold loop with left thumb.

2 Insert needle through appliqué, ¼" (6 mm) from edge, catching throw, and bring needle up at edge of appliqué, passing through the loop as shown. Pull needle through the fabric; release thumb from loop, and pull stitch tight.

3 Make second stitch ¼" (6 mm) from first stitch, as in steps 1 and 2; work stitches from right to left.

HOLIDAY PLACEMATS & NAPKINS

For a festive place setting at the table, make a set of quilted placemats that portray a winter landscape. A round napkin, folded to represent an evergreen tree, completes the setting.

The placements and napkins are made from 100 percent cotton fabric, using techniques for quick construction. Narrow piping or cording trims the edges of the lined napkin, making the napkins easy to turn and press. Simple stitch-and-turn construction eliminates binding on the placemats. The trees on the placemat are secured with machine-blindstitched appliqué.

The finished placemats measure about 12" × 18" (30.5 × 46 cm).

MATERIALS (for six placemats and napkins)

- ⅔ yd. (0.63 m) fabric, for sky section.
- ¾ yd. (0.7 m) fabric, for lower ground section of placement.
- ½ yd. (0.5 m) fabric, for upper ground section.
- 1⅛ yd. (1.05 m) fabric, for backing.
- 1½ yd. (1.4 m) each of two coordinating fabrics, for napkins and appliquéd trees on placemat.
- 9½ yd. (8.7 m) cording or piping, for trim on napkin.
- Cardboard, spray starch, and monofilament nylon thread, for blindstitched appliqués.
- Low-loft quilt batting.

CUTTING DIRECTIONS

Cut the fabric for the napkins as on page 74, step l.

Make the pattern for the placement and cut the fabric for the sky and ground pieces as on pages 75 and 76, steps 1 to 4. For each place-mat, cut one 12½" × 18½" (31.8 × 47.3 cm) rectangle from backing fabric, and one 14" × 20" (35.5 × 51 cm) rectangle from batting.

Transfer tree templates for appliqués (pages 124 and 125) onto cardboard; cut. Using templates, cut one of each tree for each placemat, adding ¼" (6 mm) seam allowances when cutting.

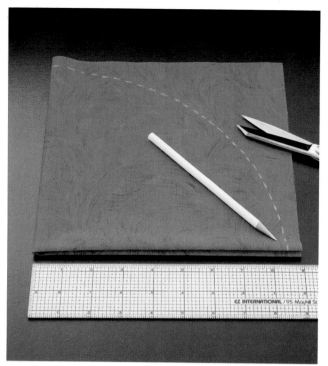

1 Cut one 18" (46 cm) square from fabric; fold in half lengthwise, then crosswise. Using a straightedge and pencil, mark an arc on the fabric, measuring 8½" (21.8 cm) from the folded center of fabric. Cut on the marked line through all layers. Using circle as pattern, cut six circles from each of the two napkin fabrics.

2 Pin trim to right side of one napkin piece, with raw edges even; curve ends of trim into seam allowance as shown, so ends overlap and trim tapers to raw edge. Machine-baste trim in place, using a zipper foot.

3 Place the napkin and lining right sides together, matching raw edges; pin. Stitch around the napkin, stitching just inside the previous stitches, crowding stitches against the trim; leave a 2" (5 cm) opening. Trim the seam allowance, using pinking shears.

4 Turn the napkin right side out; press. Edgestitch around napkin, using zipper foot and stitching opening closed.

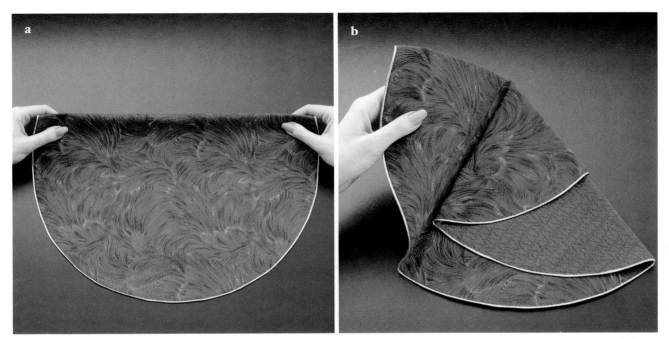

5 Fold under upper one-third of napkin **(a).** Fold right side over, then left side over, folding napkin into thirds **(b).**

HOW TO MAKE A LANDSCAPE PLACEMAT

1 Cut piece of paper 12" × 18" (30.5 × 46 cm). On left side of paper, make a mark 2½" and 9" (6.5 and 23 cm) from lower edge as shown. On right side of paper, mark 7½" (19.3 cm) from lower edge as shown.

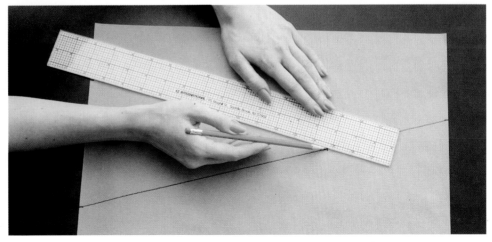

2 Draw a diagonal line connecting lower left mark to right mark as shown. Mark point on diagonal line 12" (30.5 cm) from left edge of the paper; draw a line connecting this point to the remaining mark on the left side.

(Continued)

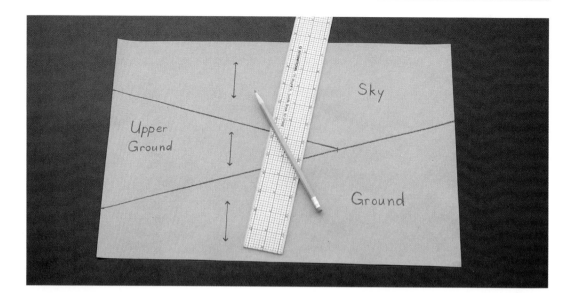

3 Label pattern sections for ground and sky, as shown; mark the grainline on each section.

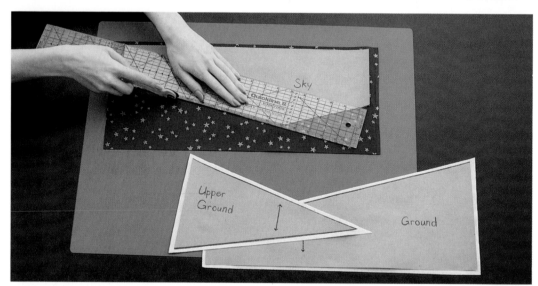

4 Cut pattern on marked lines. For each placemat, cut one of each piece from fabric, adding ¼" (6 mm) seam allowances to each side of pattern.

5 Mark each section on the wrong side of the fabric where ¼" (6 mm) seams will intersect. Align the upper ground piece and the sky piece, right sides together, matching markings for seam intersections. Stitch ¼" (6 mm) seam. Finger-press seam allowances toward upper edge of the placemat.

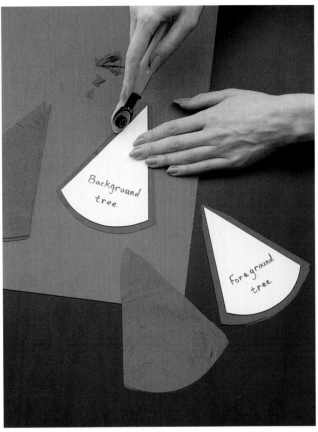

6 Align pieced unit and remaining ground piece, right sides together, matching markings for the seam intersections. Stitch ¼" (6 mm) seam. Press seam allowances toward upper edge of placemat.

7 Cut tree appliqués from fabric (page 73). Center tree templates on wrong side of fabric pieces. Trim points.

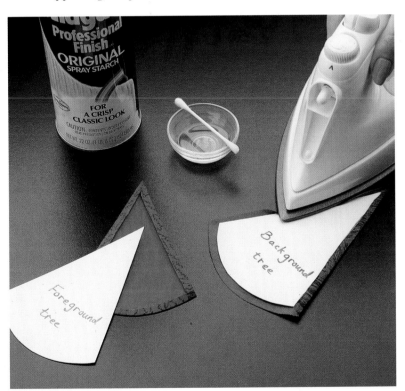

8 Spray starch into small bowl; dab starch on a section of the seam allowance. Using tip of dry iron, press seam allowance over edge of template. Continue around appliqués. Remove templates; press pieces, right side up.

9 Arrange trees on right side of pieced placemat top. Glue-baste background tree in place. Mark placement of foreground tree, using chalk; set aside.

(Continued)

10 Blindstitch around the outer edge of background tree, using monofilament nylon thread in the needle; stitch as close to the edge as possible, just catching the appliqué with the widest swing of blindstitch. Glue-baste the foreground tree in place; blindstitch. (Contrasting thread was used to show detail.)

11 Place backing and placemat top right sides together. Place fabrics on batting, with backing piece on top; pin or baste the layers together.

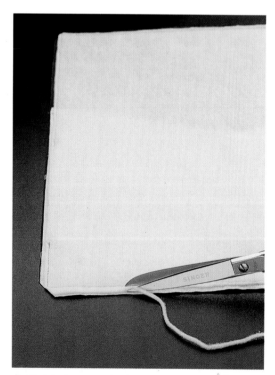

12 Stitch around placemat top, ¼" (6 mm) from the raw edges; leave 4" (10 cm) opening for turning. Trim batting to ⅛" (3 mm); trim corners.

13 Turn placemat right side out; press. Slipstitch opening closed. Quilt placemat by stitching around appliqués and on seamlines, using matching thread. Topstitch ¼" (6 mm) around outside edges. (Contrasting thread was used to show detail.)

MORE IDEAS FOR THE TABLE

Motifs *cut from printed fabric are fused to a solid background to make an interesting table covering. Simply fuse motifs to background fabric, using fusible web; then conceal cut edges of fabric, using acrylic craft paints in fine-tip tubes.*

Ribbon, *wrapped package-style around a table, creates a holiday atmosphere. Secure the ribbon in place on the underside of the table, using masking tape.*

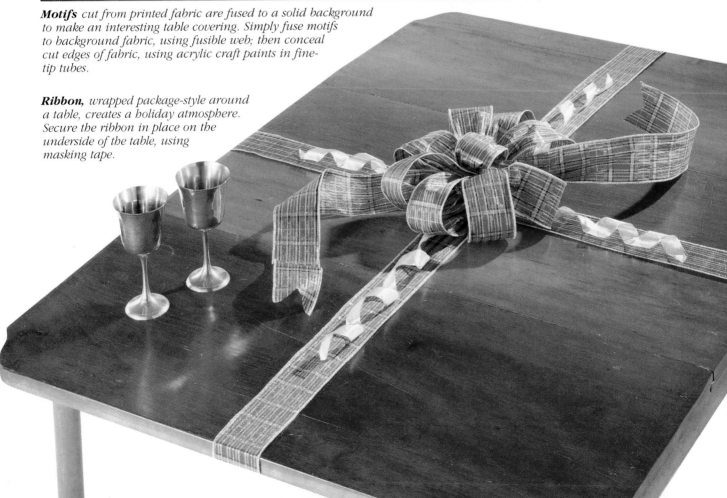

HOLIDAY FLORAL ARRANGEMENTS

Use this unique floral arrangement to add color to your holiday table. Make the arrangement from the floral materials shown, or select floral materials to coordinate with your decorating scheme.

To help create the elegant natural look of the arrangement, the preserved leaves are highlighted with gold paint. Try this simple highlighting technique on other floral materials to achieve interesting effects. The gold highlights complement the gilded terra-cotta pots that are used for the base of the arrangement.

MATERIALS

- Two terra-cotta pots, about 5" (12.5 cm) in diameter.
- Gold aerosol paint, plus optional second color.
- Floral foam, for silk arranging.
- Artificial pine boughs.

- Latex grape clusters and apples; dried pomegranates.
- 3 yd. (2.75 m) stiff decorative cording.
- Artificial or preserved leaves on branches; twigs.
- Hot glue gun and glue sticks.

HOW TO MAKE A HOLIDAY FLORAL ARRANGEMENT

1 Place a sheet of plastic on a tabletop. Spray a generous pool of aerosol paint onto the plastic; drag the preserved leaves through the paint to gild them. Allow to dry. Repeat with additional paint colors, if desired.

2 Place one pot on its side, next to the other; secure pots together, using hot glue. When dry, apply gold aerosol paint to the containers.

(Continued)

3 Cut floral foam, using knife, so it fits container snugly and is even with edge of container; secure with hot glue. Repeat for remaining container.

4 Insert pine boughs and leaf branches into foam, so they rise from 5" to 8" (12.5 to 20.5 cm) above foam. Cut pine branches into small pieces to fill area around edges of containers. Insert a few twigs into vertical pot.

5 Insert apples and grape clusters, allowing some of the grapes to cascade slightly over sides of containers. Secure pomegranates into arrangement as desired with hot glue.

6 Apply tape to decorative braid at 8" to 12" (20.5 to 30.5 cm) intervals; cut braid through center of tape. Form loops from lengths of braid; wrap ends together with tape. Insert loops of decorative braid into arrangement, securing braid to foam with hot glue.

WALL TREES

Make a stunning wall accent from a miniature artificial pine tree. The branches of the tree are bent to the front, creating a flat surface in the back. This allows the tree to be displayed flat against a wall. The wall tree is embellished with a variety of fruit and is topped with a large bow.

MATERIALS

- Artificial pine tree with attached trunk, about 24" (61 cm) tall.
- Four or five varieties of fruit, including apples, pears, grape clusters, and berries.
- Preserved leaves on stems.
- 3 yd. (2.75 m) wired ribbon, for bow.
- Floral wire.

1 Bend branches of artificial tree around to one side. Place flat on table, and arrange branches.

2 Secure pears to tree with hot glue, forming a curved diagonal line as shown.

3 Gild leaves as on page 81, step 1. Secure thin layer of gilded leaves along sides of pears, using hot glue. Lift pine boughs to surround the row of pears and leaves. Insert second variety of fruit and another row of gilded leaves, following the same line as the pears; secure with hot glue.

4 Continue to secure alternating rows of fruit and gilded leaves, until the entire tree is covered. Arrange pine boughs between rows of fruit and leaves.

5 Form large loops from wired ribbon as shown **(a).** Continue to make six loops. Make small loop at center. Bend wire around ribbon at center; twist wire tightly, gathering ribbon **(b).** Separate and shape the loops.

6 Secure bow to top of tree, using wire. Twist excess wire into loop at back, for hanging tree. Tuck ends of ribbon into sides of tree.

TOPIARY TREES

Make a classic topiary tree to accent your fireplace or display on a sideboard for the holidays. This finished tree measures about 24" (61 cm) tall. Embellish the top of this miniature tree with artificial fruit, floral materials, and decorative ribbon. The tree is set in a terra-cotta pot.

MATERIALS

- 4" (10 cm) Styrofoam® ball.
- Artificial pine boughs.
- Wired ribbon.
- Latex grape clusters and small pears.
- Dried yarrow.
- Small red-leaf preserved foliage; artificial green leaves.
- 7" (18 cm) terra-cotta pot.
- Floral foam, for silk arranging.
- Several dogwood stems.
- Hot glue gun and glue sticks.

1 Trim floral foam with a knife to fit pot snugly; secure with hot glue. Cut dogwood stems about 14" (35.5 cm) long. Insert several stems into center of the pot; secure with hot glue.

HOW TO MAKE A TOPIARY TREE

(Continued)

2 Secure the opposite ends of the stems to one side of the Styrofoam® ball, using hot glue.

3 Cut pine boughs into pieces about 3" (7.5 cm) long. Insert the pine stems into ball and foam in pot until the surfaces are covered.

4 Cut apart the grape stems and pears; insert as desired, securing with hot glue. Insert a large grape cluster into pot, allowing it to cascade over edge.

5 Cut red-leaf foliage into 4" (10 cm) stems. Secure leaf stems and yarrow pieces to ball with hot glue. Tuck the ribbon into ball; secure with hot glue, if necessary.

HANGING PINE BALLS

A holiday pine ball is created by decorating a Styrofoam® ball with pine stems, preserved leaves, and artificial berries. Display the pine ball indoors by hanging it from either a window or door frame, using a decorative ribbon and an upholstery tack. The pine ball can also be hung outdoors, offering a festive welcome to holiday guests.

MATERIALS

- 4" (10 cm) Styrofoam ball.
- Artificial pine boughs.
- Small-leaf preserved foliage.
- Artificial berries.
- Ribbon; floral wire.

HOW TO MAKE A HANGING PINE BALL

1 Cut several pieces of pine into 1½" (3.8 cm) lengths. Insert pine lengths into ball until surface is covered. Insert short pieces of small-leaf foliage into the ball, interspersing them among pine lengths. Cut sprigs of berries, and insert berries as desired.

2 Make six ribbon loops; secure with glue at center as shown. Cut ribbon to desired length for hanger. Cut 8" (20.5 cm) length of wire. Hold end of ribbon over wire; secure with glue. Bend wire ends down; insert wire ends into the foam ball over ribbon loops.

Gift Giving
& Cards

CANDY WREATHS

A candy wreath is a festive holiday decoration full of little gifts. In one version, brightly wrapped Christmas candies nestle among coils of curled ribbon. For a fringed fabric wreath, candies are tied with raffia between knotted strips of cotton fabric. Small scissors hanging from the wreath invite each guest to snip out a piece of candy.

MATERIALS

- Metal ring, 8" (20.5 cm) in diameter.
- 50 to 70 yd. (46 to 64.4 m) curling ribbon in choice of colors, for ribbon wreath.
- ¼ yd. (0.25 m) each of three cotton print fabrics, for fringed fabric wreath.
- Raffia, for fringed fabric wreath.
- Wrapped Christmas candies.
- Small scissors.

HOW TO MAKE A CANDY & RIBBON WREATH

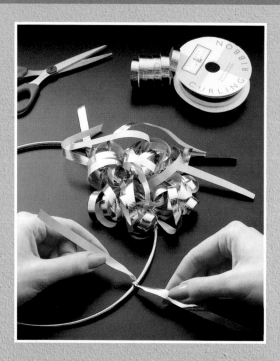

1 Cut a 12" (30.5 cm) length of curling ribbon. Wrap ribbon around metal ring; knot, leaving tails of equal length. Repeat, alternating ribbon colors as desired; cover about 4" (10 cm) of the metal ring.

2 Curl ribbon tails with blade of scissors. Tie pieces of wrapped candy to wreath; space evenly. Pack knotted ribbons tightly.

3 Repeat steps 1 and 2 until the entire wreath is covered. Fold 40" (102 cm) length of curling ribbon in half; wrap folded end around metal ring at top of wreath. Knot, allowing 2" (5 cm) loop for hanger.

4 Insert tails of ribbon through handle of small scissors; knot, allowing scissors to hang just below wreath. Curl ribbon tails.

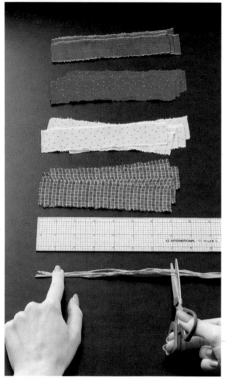

1 Cut selvages from fabrics. Tear fabric crosswise into strips, 1½" (3.8 cm) wide. Cut strips into 7" (18 cm) lengths. Cut raffia into 7" (18 cm) lengths.

2 Wrap length of fabric around metal ring; knot, leaving tails of equal length. Wrap length of raffia around metal ring next to knotted fabric; knot, leaving tails of equal length. Repeat until entire ring is covered, alternating fabrics and packing knots close together.

3 Tie wrapped candies to wreath where desired, using raffia tails.

4 Fold 36" (91.5 cm) length of raffia in half; wrap the folded end around the metal ring at top of wreath. Knot, allowing 2" (5 cm) loop for the hanger. Insert tails of raffia through the handle of a small pair of scissors; knot, allowing the scissors to hang just below wreath.

HOLIDAY COASTER SETS

As a gift for the hostess, make a set of holiday coasters and package them in a decorative box. Purchase a small cardboard box and lid in a holiday-motif shape, such as a star, heart, or tree. Make the padded coasters in the same shape as the box, using cotton quilting fabric and needlepunched cotton batting. Paint the box, and adorn the lid with an additional coaster, giving a clue to the contents of the box.

MATERIALS

- Cardboard box in holiday-motif shape, such as a star, heart, or tree, measuring about 2" (5 cm) high and 4" to 5" (10 to 12.5 cm) in diameter.
- 1/2 yd. (0.5 m) cotton quilting fabric in Christmas print.

- 1/2 yd. (0.5 m) needlepunched cotton batting.
- Pinking shears.
- Embellishments, such as tiny buttons or ribbons, optional.
- Acrylic paint and paintbrush.
- Craft glue.

HOW TO MAKE A HOLIDAY COASTER SET

1 Prewash fabric and batting, following the manufacturer's instructions. Fold fabric in half, wrong sides together, matching selvages. Trace the box bottom on right side of fabric eight times, for eight coasters; allow ½" (1.3 cm) between coasters. Trace the box lid once for larger coaster.

2 Insert batting between the layers of fabric. Secure fabric and batting layers together, using two or three pins in each traced coaster.

3 Cut coasters apart through all layers, leaving irregular margins around each coaster. Stitch layers together, using small stitches, and stitching ¼" (6 mm) inside traced lines.

4 Cut out coasters just inside traced lines, using pinking shears. Embellish the coasters with small buttons or other embellishments, if desired.

5 Paint all surfaces of cardboard box and lid, using acrylic paint and paintbrush. Allow to dry.

6 Insert the eight small coasters into box. Embellish large coaster for lid with bow or other embellishment, if desired. Secure large coaster to lid, using craft glue.

PINECONE KINDLERS
ಌ

Place kindler under
firewood and light.

HAPPY HOLIDAYS

PINECONE KINDLERS

For an inexpensive gift that is both useful and decorative, fill a basket with pinecone kindlers. Pinecones are dipped in melted paraffin wax and cooled in metal or glass muffin cups atop shallow paraffin wax bases. Candlewicks running through the bases keep the pinecones burning for up to twenty minutes, while kindling logs for the fire. Paraffin for the pinecone kindlers can be colored red and scented with cinnamon, or colored green and scented with pine, if desired. To light a fire, center a pinecone kindler under stacked firewood and light the wick.

MATERIALS

- Double boiler.
- Paraffin wax, approximately 1 lb. (450 g) per six pinecones.
- Candle color squares and candle scent squares, one square each per pound (450 g) of paraffin wax.
- Candy thermometer.
- Muffin tin.
- Nonstick vegetable oil spray.
- Wax-coated candlewicks, 6" (15 cm) long.
- Pinecones, 2" (5 cm) in diameter or size to fit muffin cups.
- Tongs.

HOW TO MAKE PINECONE KINDLERS

1 Insert candy thermometer into double boiler. Melt one pound (450 g) paraffin wax in top of double boiler over boiling water. Add one square of the candle color and one square of candle scent as desired. Mix gently, using wooden spoon.

2 Spray the muffin cups lightly with nonstick vegetable oil spray. Place one end of wax-coated candlewick in each muffin cup; allow opposite end to hang over side of muffin cup.

3 Cool melted paraffin to about 160°F (70°C). Dip pinecone in paraffin, turning to coat thoroughly. Raise pinecone above wax for a few seconds, allowing parafin to harden; repeat two or three times. Remove with tongs, and place coated pinecone upright in muffin cup over candlewick.

4 Remove top pan of double boiler containing remaining melted paraffin. Dry outside of pan with towel to prevent water from dripping into muffin cups. Slowly pour ½" (1.3 cm) melted paraffin into each muffin cup at base of pinecone.

5 Allow the kindlers to cool completely. Remove from muffin cups. Arrange in decorative gift basket; prepare note card with instructions for use.

LOG CARRIERS

Make a sturdy log carrier to fill with firewood and give as a gift. The log carrier is made from medium-weight to heavyweight fabric, such as upholstery fabric or denim, and lined with cotton duck. The durable wooden dowel handles are easy to grasp, and the bottom gussets prevent twigs and debris from falling out of the carrier.

MATERIALS

- 1¼ yd. (1.15 m) mediumweight to heavyweight fabric, such as upholstery fabric or denim, for outer fabric.
- 1¼ yd. (1.15 m) cotton duck fabric, for lining.
- Dowel, ¾" (2 cm) diameter, 48" (122 cm) length.

CUTTING DIRECTIONS

Make the pattern as in steps 1 to 4, below. Cut one log carrier piece from the outer fabric and one from the lining. Cut the dowel into two 24" (61 cm) lengths.

HOW TO MAKE A
LOG CARRIER PATTERN

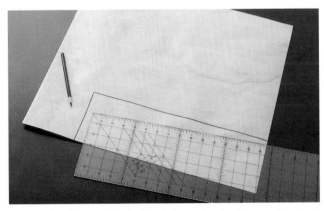

1 Cut large paper rectangle to measure 36½" × 42" (92.8 × 107 cm). Fold rectangle in half lengthwise; fold in half again crosswise, to get a folded rectangle measuring 18¼" × 21" (46.6 × 53.5 cm).

2 Draw a line, 16" (40.5 cm) long, beginning at short cut edges, parallel to and 5" (12.5 cm) away from the long cut edges. Draw a perpendicular line from end of 16" (40.5 cm) line to long cut edges.

(Continued)

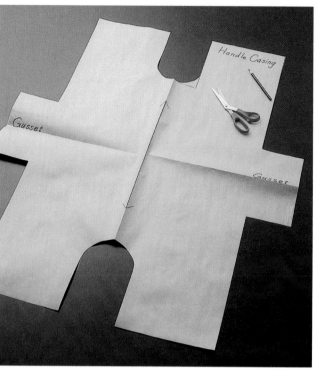

3 Draw a line, 9" (23 cm) long, beginning at short cut edges, parallel to and 3" (7.5 cm) away from long fold. Draw a perpendicular line from end of 9" (23 cm) line to long fold. Round the inner corner, using a saucer as shown.

4 Cut on lines through all layers; unfold pattern. Label grainline on long center fold. Label handle casings and gussets as shown.

HOW TO MAKE A LOG CARRIER

1 Press under ½" (1.3 cm) on one handle casing of outer fabric; repeat for lining.

2 Pin outer fabric to lining, right sides together, matching the raw edges and pressed folds. Stitch ½" (1.3 cm) from edges, leaving an opening at pressed folds.

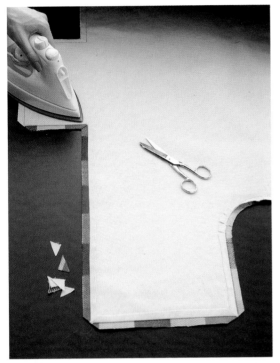

3 Trim outer corners diagonally; clip the inner corners to stitches, and clip curves. Press the lining seam allowance toward lining.

4 Turn right side out through the opening; press the seamed edges. Fold 2" (5 cm) to the wrong side on all four handle casings; pin. Stitch close to the seamed edges of three finished casings; stitch again ¼" (6 mm) from the seamed edges. At handle casing with opening, stitch through all layers, close to the folds, closing opening; stitch again ¼" (6 mm) from folds.

5 Pin gusset to side of log carrier, wrong sides together, matching seamed edges. Stitch close to seamed edges, backstitching to secure; stitch again ¼" (6 mm) from seamed edges. Repeat for remaining gusset seams.

6 Paint handles as desired, or stain handles and apply clear acrylic finish; allow to dry. Insert handles into handle casings.

WOODEN BASKETS

Handcrafted wooden baskets are ideal for gift giving and can be used as decorative accents throughout the holiday season. Make the baskets using either a snowman or a Christmas tree design. An aged look, achieved by sanding the edges and applying stain, gives the baskets a rustic charm. They are inexpensive to make and require only basic woodworking skills and tools.

When cutting with a jigsaw, it is helpful to clamp the wood in place, protecting it with wood scraps or felt pads, if necessary. This also allows you to hold the saw firmly with both hands, to reduce vibration, and move the saw smoothly while cutting. Cut inside corners by sawing into the corner from both directions; cut curves slowly to avoid bending the blade.

MATERIALS

- 12 ft. (3.7 m) of 1/4" × 3/4" (6 mm × 2 cm) pine screen molding.
- 1 × 8 pine board.
- Wooden dowel, 1/2" (1.3 cm) diameter, 11 1/4" (28.7 cm) long.
- Jigsaw.
- Drill; 1/16" and 1/2" drill bits.
- Sanding block; medium-grit and fine-grit sandpaper.
- Acrylic paints; artist's brushes.
- Stain in medium color, such as medium walnut.
- 17 × 3/4" (2 cm) brads.
- Wood glue; tracing paper; graphite paper.
- Scrap of wool fabric, for snowman scarf, optional.

HOW TO MAKE A WOODEN BASKET

1 Fold sheet of tracing paper in half lengthwise. Trace the partial pattern (page 125) for tree or snowman onto tracing paper, placing fold of tracing paper on dotted line of pattern. Cut out pattern. Open the full-size pattern. Transfer the pattern to 1 × 8 pine board twice, using graphite paper; align the arrow on pattern with grain of wood. Transfer mark for handle.

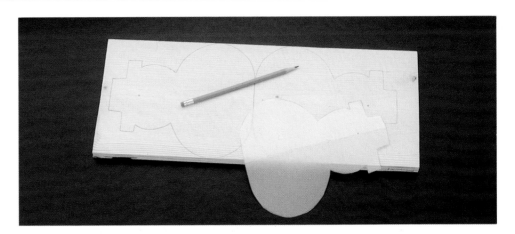

(Continued)

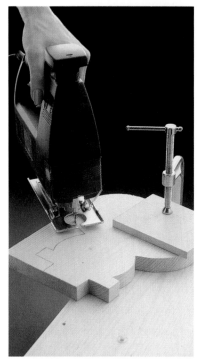

2 Cut along marked lines, using jigsaw.

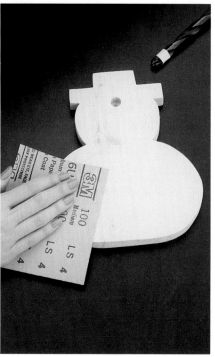

3 Drill hole at mark for handle to ³⁄₈" (1 cm) depth, using ½" drill bit; use masking tape on drill bit as guide for the depth. Sand basket ends smooth, using medium-grit sandpaper.

4 Mark and cut twelve slats from screen molding, in 12" (30.5 cm) lengths. Sand ends. Predrill nail holes ³⁄₈" (1 cm) from each end of each slat, using ¹⁄₁₆" drill bit.

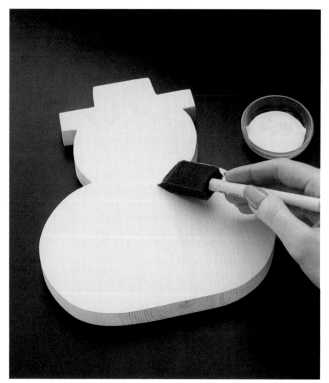

5 Paint outer surface of basket ends as desired, using acrylic paints and foam applicator. Allow to dry.

6 Sand edges of the basket ends lightly, using fine-grit sandpaper, to remove some paint and give an aged appearance.

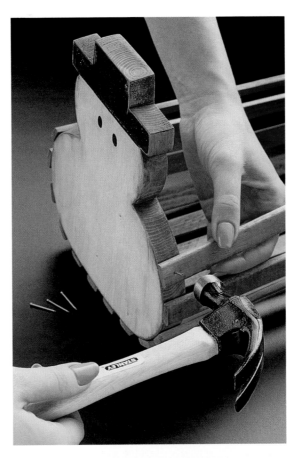

7 Apply stain to all pieces, using soft cloth; allow to dry.

8 Mark placement for slats on the basket ends, using pattern as guide. Secure slats to one basket end, using 17 × 3/4" (2 cm) brads; align the end of slat to outer edge of basket end, with the rounded edges of the slat facing outward.

9 Apply small amount of wood glue in the holes for handle. Insert dowel ends into holes.

10 Secure slats to remaining basket end. For snowman basket, cut two 1½" × 22" (3.8 × 56 cm) fabric strips; clip ends to make fringe, and tie around necks, for scarves.

QUICK & EASY GIFT IDEAS

For handcrafted gifts that are simple to make, try a delicate Christmas potpourri, an herbal cooking oil, or a decorative painted candle. For potpourri, use the recipe opposite for a mixture with a dominant pine scent. Or vary the floral elements and use an essential oil of your choice. When varying the recipe, always remember to use a fixative, since this is the ingredient that helps the potpourri retain its scent.

Herbal cooking oil can easily be made in a few minutes; however, it must sit for about three weeks before it can be used. To help distribute the flavor, shake the bottle every few days. The flavor becomes stronger, the longer it sits.

Easy-to-make painted candles can become personalized gifts. Decorate them with Christmas motifs, favorite verses from Christmas carols, or personal names.

Painted candles (opposite) are decorated in the holiday spirit. Select pillar candles with smooth surfaces, and embellish as desired with craft acrylic paints. Add dimensional detail with acrylic paints in fine-tip tubes. Or add sparkle with glitter glue.

Herbal cooking oils (right) are great gift ideas for the cooking enthusiast. Wash and dry fresh herbs, such as rosemary, tarragon, thyme, basil, or dill; then place about three sprigs of the selected herb in a decorative bottle. Fill the bottle with a cooking oil, such as olive oil or corn oil; then cap the bottle with a cork and allow to sit at room temperature for about three weeks. Homemade cooking oils should be used immediately when ready. Keep oil stored in the refrigerator.

CHRISTMAS POTPOURRI

1 qt. (1 L) mixture of small pinecones, star anise, juniper berries, red rose petals, green eucalyptus, and cedar needles.

10 to 15 red rose heads or buds.

10 to 12 cinnamon sticks, 3" (7.5 cm) long.

½ teaspoon (2 mL) whole cloves.

Four drops pine essential oil.

Two drops cinnamon essential oil.

Fixative, such as 1 oz. (25 g) orris root powder or ¼ cup (50 mL) cut orris root, chopped calamus, or cellulose-fiber fixative.

Place fixative in bowl and add drops of essential oils. Mix thoroughly, to ensure that scent of oil is fixed. Mix remaining ingredients in large bowl. Add fixative and essential oil mixture to large bowl; mix thoroughly. Place potpourri in airtight container; leave in dark place for at least six weeks. Shake container daily for first week. Package potpourri in a decorative canister to give as a gift, or keep it yourself and display in a decorative open container.

Christmas potpourri (below) makes a decorative room accent and provides a pleasant aroma.

FABRIC GIFT WRAPS

Wrap packages creatively with fabric gift wraps. Choose from three styles, including circular gift wraps, rolled gift wraps, or gift bags. Make the gift wraps from lightweight to mediumweight fabrics, such as satin, taffeta, lamé, or seasonal broadcloth prints. Line the gift wraps with contrasting fabrics; the wraps can then be reversed and used with different trimmings for a new look for the following year. Embellish the gift wraps with coordinating trims, such as wired ribbon or cording. Purchased end caps may be applied to the ends of the cording, if desired.

The circular gift wrap is ideal for baked goods and soft garment accessories, such as slippers, mittens, or socks. The rolled gift wrap works well for soft gift items, such as articles of clothing, that can be folded into rectangles. Custom-sized gift bags can be used for bottles and other items that are difficult to wrap.

CUTTING DIRECTIONS

For the circular gift wrap, cut one circle each from outer fabric and lining as on page 112, steps 1 and 2.

For the rolled gift wrap, cut one rectangle each from outer fabric and lining, 4" (10 cm) larger than gift on all sides.

For the gift bag, cut two rectangles each from outer fabric and lining, using the method on page 113, step 1, to determine the size of the rectangles.

MATERIALS

- Fabrics, for gift wrap and contrasting lining.
- Rubber band.
- Ribbon or cording.
- End caps, for cording, optional.

HOW TO SEW A CIRCULAR GIFT WRAP

1 Position the gift as it will placed in center of gift wrap. Determine diameter of the circle by measuring around the gift as shown and adding 4" to 10" (10 to 25 cm) for heading and seam allowances.

2 Fold outer fabric in half lengthwise, then crosswise. Using a straightedge and pencil, mark an arc on fabric, measuring one-half desired diameter of circle from folded center of fabric. Cut on marked line through all layers; mark raw edge at foldlines. Cut lining to same size; mark.

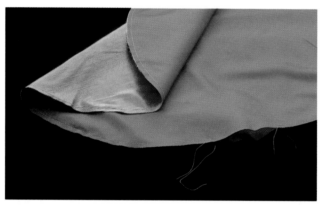

3 Pin the outer fabric to lining, right sides together, matching marks; stitch ¼" (6 mm) from raw edges, leaving 4" (10 cm) opening for turning.

4 Turn right side out; press. Slipstitch opening closed. Center the gift on the fabric. Draw fabric around gift, securing it with rubber band. Adjust folds; tie ribbon or cording around top, concealing rubber band.

HOW TO SEW A ROLLED GIFT WRAP

1 Pin outer fabric to lining, right sides together, stitch ¼" (6 mm) from raw edges, leaving 4" (10 cm) opening for turning.

2 Turn the rectangle right side out; press. Slipstitch the opening closed. Center gift on fabric, allowing space around all sides. Roll up rectangle.

3 Draw up fabric at ends, securing it with rubber bands. Adjust folds; tie cording or ribbon around ends, concealing rubber band.

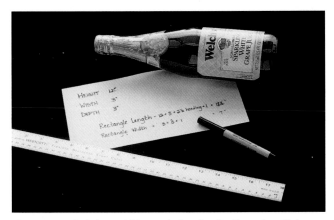

1 Measure height, width, and depth of gift as it will be inserted in the gift bag; record these measurements. Determine the size of rectangles for gift bag, with length equal to height and depth of gift plus desired heading plus 1" (2.5 cm); width of rectangle is equal to width and depth of gift plus 1" (2.5 cm).

2 Cut rectangles from the outer fabric and lining as determined in step 1. Pin the rectangles right sides together; stitch ¼" (6 mm) from raw edges, leaving top of gift bag open. Repeat for lining, leaving 3" (7.5 cm) opening on one side near top.

3 Fold gift bag at bottom so side seam is aligned to the bottom seam; pin. Measure from the corner across seams a distance equal to one-half the depth of the gift; mark a point on seamline. Draw a line through point, perpendicular to seamline.

4 Stitch along marked line; trim close to the stitching. Repeat steps 3 and 4 for opposite corner, and repeat for corners of lining.

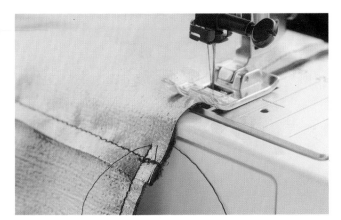

5 Place outer bag inside the lining, right sides together. Pin upper edges, raw edges even; stitch ¼" (6 mm) from edge. Turn right side out through opening in lining. Hand-stitch opening closed.

6 Insert lining; lightly press upper edge. Insert the gift into bag; draw fabric up around gift, securing it with a rubber band. Tie ribbon or cording around top, concealing rubber band.

RIBBON GIFT-BOWS

Packages wrapped with lavish bows make beautiful displays beneath the tree and entice the gift recipient. Ribbon gift-bows are simple to make and suitable for many types of ribbon, including wired ribbon, sinamay ribbon, paper twist, and metallic twist.

The bow is assembled using a stapler. For best results, use a hand stapler. This style stapler, available at office supply stores, allows you to secure the ribbon snugly around the box. Each bow requires about 2½ yd. (2.3 m) of ribbon, plus the amount needed to wrap around the box.

When selecting papers, think beyond the typical wrapping papers. Papers such as plain white and brown paper, printed newspaper, parchment paper, and decorative tissue papers make packages unique. Materials such as corrugated cardboard, fabric, and cellophane can also be used. For additional embellishment, personalize the package with an ornament or sprig of greenery.

MATERIALS

- Ribbon.
- Hand stapler.

HOW TO MAKE A RIBBON GIFT-BOW

1 Wrap ribbon around box in one direction; secure with staple. Trim excess ribbon.

2 Form ribbon into a 5½" to 6" (14 to 15 cm) loop as shown, allowing about an 8" (20.5 cm) tail and taking care that the right side of the ribbon is facing out.

3 Fold a loop toward the opposite side, bringing ribbon over tail to keep right side of ribbon facing out.

5 Tie about a 24" (61 cm) length of ribbon around center of bow, knotting it on back of bow. Trim tails as desired.

4 Continue wrapping ribbon to form two loops on each side with a second tail extending. Position bow over ribbon on package; secure with one or two staples at center.

QUICK & EASY GIFT WRAPPING

For unique gift wrapping, personalize a variety of simple bags or containers. Choose from buckets, pine bandboxes, lunch bags, or shopping bags. These types of packaging can often be kept for future use. Embellish the packaging with painted designs, stickers, floral materials, or even a keepsake ornament.

Personalized gift wrap *is easy to create. Above, the tin bucket is painted to make a keepsake container for a child's gift. Lunch bags, embellished with stickers, become personalized packages, and holiday shoelaces replace a traditional ribbon on a Christmas gift. Opposite, a bandbox is embellished with a cluster of ribbon roses (page 37), for a romantic package. Beeswax ornaments, made by pouring melted wax into cookie molds, decorate a plain brown-paper gift bag. Wine-bottle bag, sprayed with silver and gold paint, becomes an instant gift bag. Cardboard tubes, concealing small gifts, are wrapped to represent Christmas "firecrackers."*

FIBER-MÂCHÉ CARDS & GIFT TAGS

Create unique cards or gift tags, using a fiber-mâché arts and crafts medium, such as WildFiber™. This material is composed of natural and synthetic fibers, and a non-toxic binder. When combined with water, the fibers adhere to each other, allowing the mixture to be molded or rolled flat to create a substance with the look of handmade paper. WildFiber is available in a wide range of colors at many arts and crafts stores. For dimensional designs, WildFiber can be pressed into plastic molds. Or to create your own flat images, roll the material flat between plastic sheets; allow it to dry. Then cut or tear your own shapes. Use the fiber-mâché shapes as gift tags, or glue them to blank greeting cards to make custom-designed Christmas cards. Blank greeting cards can be found at stationery or office supply stores.

MATERIALS

- Fiber-mâché, such as WildFiber, in desired colors.
- Bowl; craft sticks.
- Paper toweling.
- Plastic-wrapped cardboard, extra plastic.
- Metal cookie cutter, for shapes with torn edges.
- Rolling pin.
- Plastic molds.
- Narrow ribbon or cording, for gift tag; darning needle.
- Craft glue.

HOW TO MAKE MOLDED FIBER-MÂCHÉ CARDS & GIFT TAGS

1 Mix WildFiber with water to create a pastelike consistency. Allow to set 15 minutes, until moisture has been absorbed by fibers.

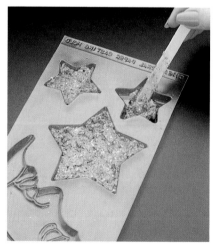

2 Spread and press mixture on the inside surface of the mold with a craft stick, until about 1/8" (3 mm) thick. Place mold in freezer for about 30 minutes to set shape.

3 Carefully remove molded shape from mold; place on several sheets of paper toweling until dry. Secure to blank gift card or piece of decorative paper, using glue. For gift tag, thread cording or narrow ribbon into darning needle; then insert through top of tag, and knot ends.

HOW TO MAKE FLAT FIBER-MÂCHÉ CARDS & GIFT TAGS

1 Mix WildFiber as in step 1, opposite. Place WildFiber mixture between a piece of plastic-wrapped cardboard and a second piece of plastic; then roll it out to desired thickness with rolling pin. Place in freezer for about 30 minutes. Remove from freezer; let set for 5 minutes.

2 Press imprint of desired shape into fiber-mâché. Allow to dry. Tear or cut along imprint line. Secure to blank gift card or piece of decorative paper, using glue. For gift tag, thread cording or narrow ribbon into darning needle; then insert through top of tag, and knot ends.

CARDS & GIFT TAGS

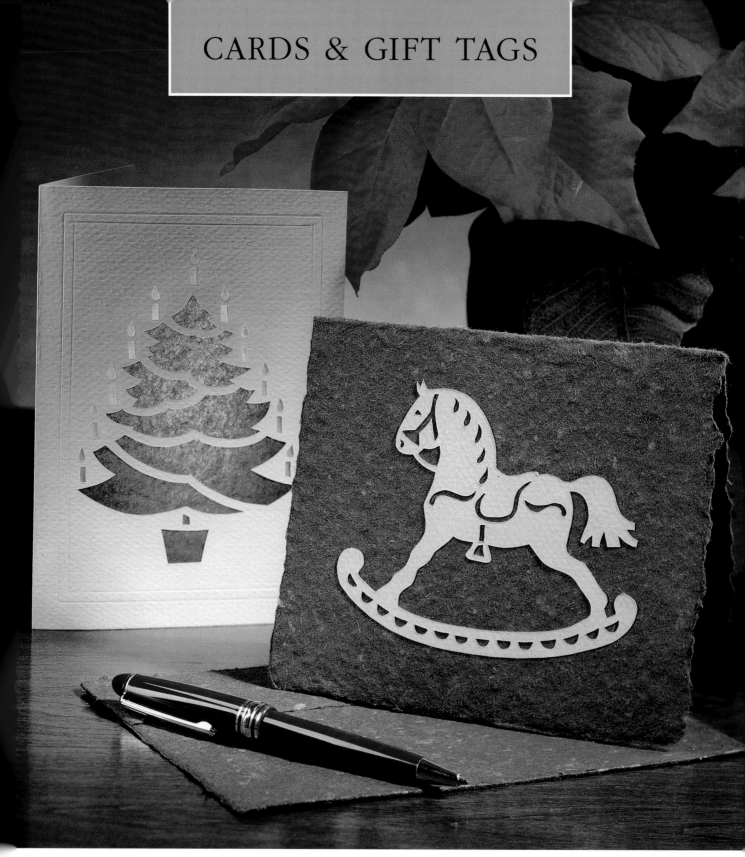

Personalized cards and gift tags can easily be made from card stock and heavyweight stationery. Or use blank greeting cards with matching envelopes, available at stationery or office supply stores. Christmas ornaments are perfect for gift tags, since they become an extra keepsake gift.

Scherenschnitte card *is created by securing an ornament (page 13) to card-stock paper, using aerosol adhesive.*

Christmas tree cutout card *is made from a blank greeting card. The design is cut in the front of the card, using a mat knife; then tissue paper is glued to the back of the cutout for a translucent effect.*

Felt ornament reindeer *(above) cleverly displays a small gift tag, while embellishing the top of a package.*

Wooden cutout *(above, right) is painted with craft acrylic paint to make a gift tag.*

Hand-cast paper gift tag *(below) is made from a hand-cast paper ornament (page 20). Secure the ornament to handmade paper, using craft glue.*

To: Lori

To: Carol
From: Mom

To Lisa
From Mark

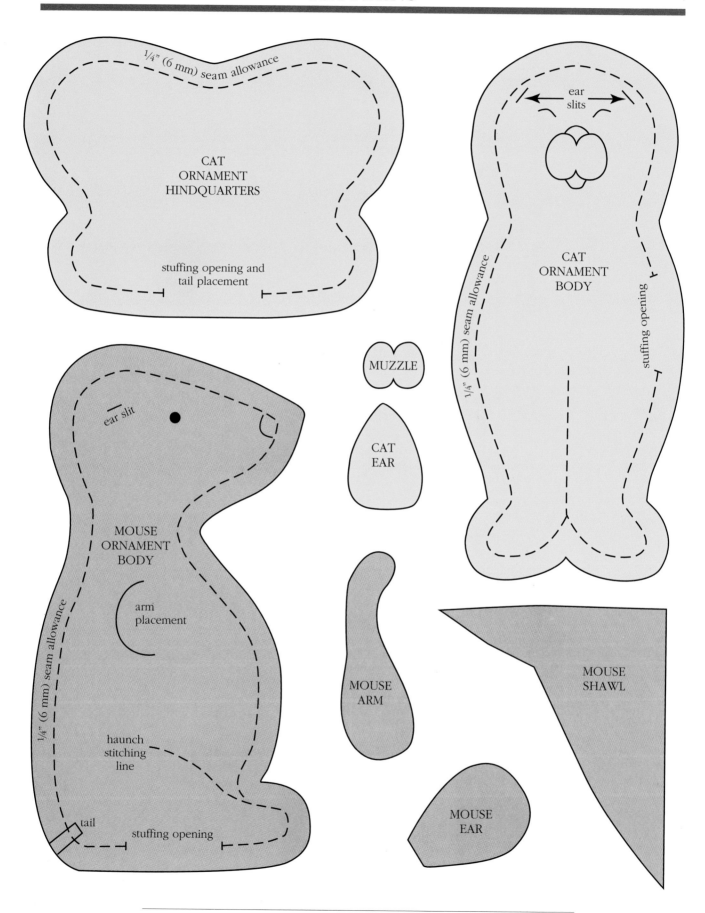

CAT
ORNAMENT
HINDQUARTERS

¼" (6 mm) seam allowance

stuffing opening and
tail placement

ear
slits

CAT
ORNAMENT
BODY

¼" (6 mm) seam allowance

stuffing opening

MUZZLE

CAT
EAR

ear slit

MOUSE
ORNAMENT
BODY

arm
placement

¼" (6 mm) seam allowance

haunch
stitching
line

tail

stuffing opening

MOUSE
ARM

MOUSE
SHAWL

MOUSE
EAR

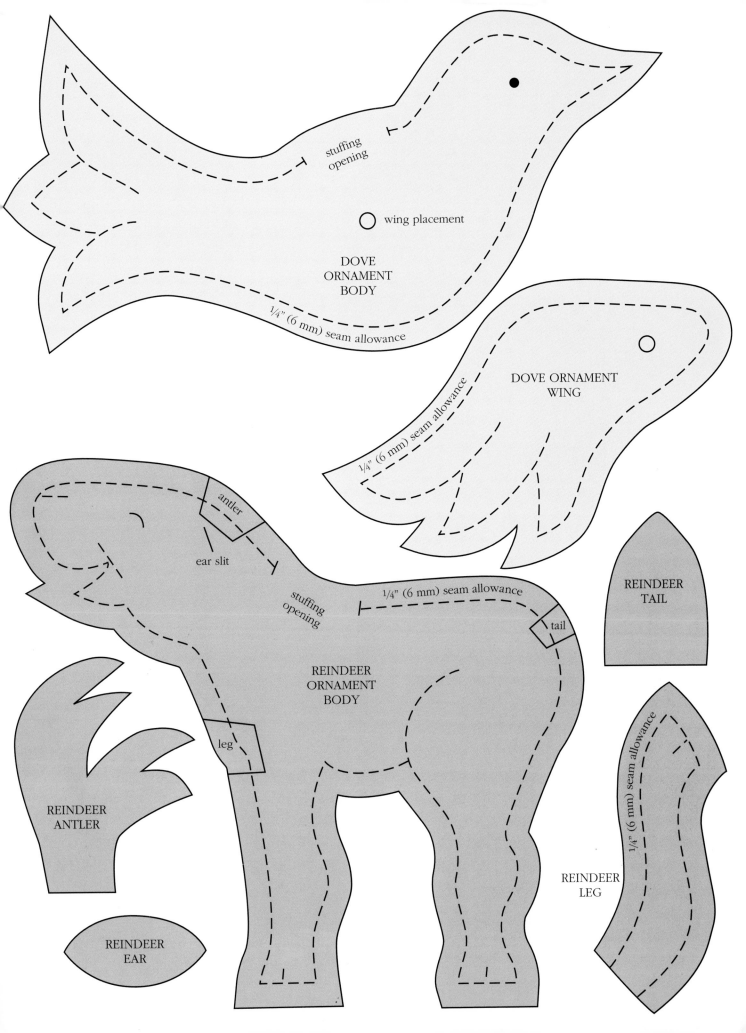

stuffing
opening

wing placement

DOVE
ORNAMENT
BODY

1/4" (6 mm) seam allowance

DOVE ORNAMENT
WING

1/4" (6 mm) seam allowance

antler

ear slit

stuffing
opening

1/4" (6 mm) seam allowance

tail

REINDEER
TAIL

REINDEER
ORNAMENT
BODY

leg

1/4" (6 mm) seam allowance

REINDEER
ANTLER

REINDEER
LEG

REINDEER
EAR

BACKGROUND TREE TEMPLATE
FOR HOLIDAY PLACEMATS

DOVE GARLAND

Place on fold

Place on fold

ROCKING HORSE ORNAMENT
Dimensions 3½" × 4¼" (9 × 10.8 cm)

PACKAGE
ORNAMENT
Dimensions
4⅝" × 3½"
(11.7 × 9 cm)

Place on fold

Place on fold

CANDLE
ORNAMENT
Dimensions
4¼" × 3¼" (10.8 × 8.2 cm)

Dimensions
6⅛" × 6¾"
(15.4 × 17 cm)

PARTRIDGE
ORNAMENT

Place on fold

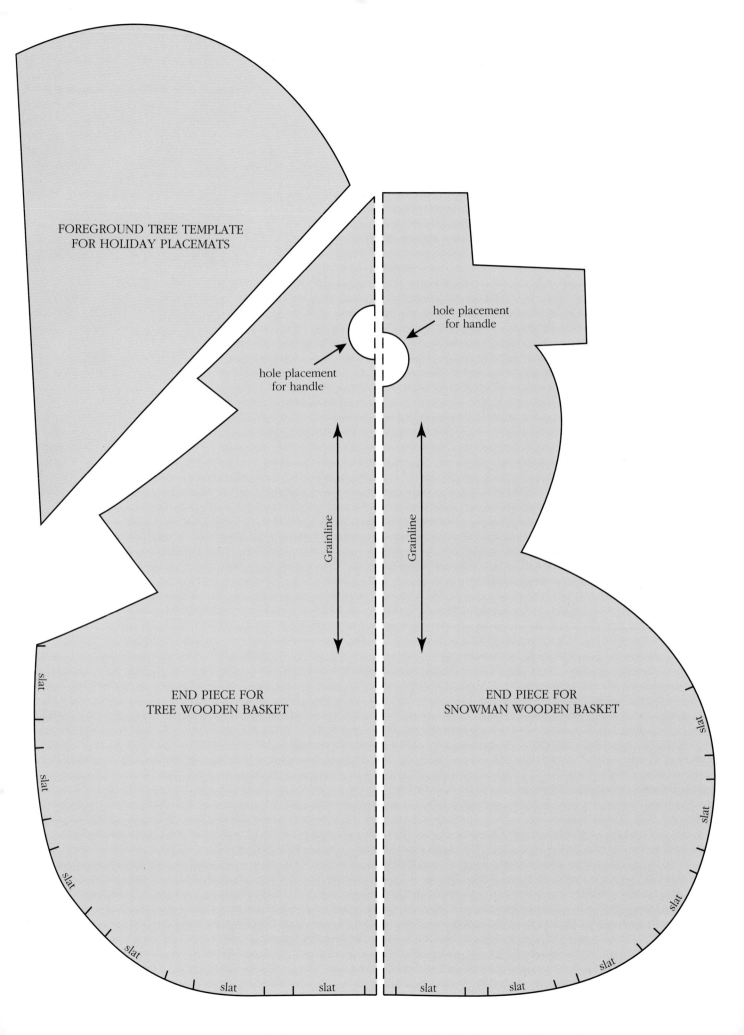

FOREGROUND TREE TEMPLATE
FOR HOLIDAY PLACEMATS

hole placement
for handle

hole placement
for handle

Grainline

Grainline

END PIECE FOR
TREE WOODEN BASKET

END PIECE FOR
SNOWMAN WOODEN BASKET

slat

slat

slat

slat

slat

slat

slat

slat

slat

slat

slat

slat

INDEX

CREDITS

President: Iain Macfarlane

THE GIFT OF CHRISTMAS
Created by: The Editors of
Creative Publishing international, Inc.

Books available in this series:
*Bedroom Decorating, Creative Window
Treatments, Decorating for Christmas,
Decorating the Living Room, Creative
Accessories for the Home, Decorating with
Silk & Dried Flowers, Kitchen & Bathroom
Ideas, Decorating the Kitchen, Decorative
Painting, Decorating Your Home for
Christmas, Decorating for Dining &
Entertaining, Decorating with Fabric &
Wallcovering, Decorating the Bathroom,
Decorating with Great Finds, Affordable
Decorating, Picture-Perfect Walls, More
Creative Window Treatments, Outdoor
Decor, The Gift of Christmas, Home
Accents in a Flash, Painted Illusions,
Halloween Decorating, 'Tis the Season*

Group Executive Editor: Zoe A. Graul
Editorial Manager: Dawn M. Anderson
Project Manager: Elaine Johnson
Associate Creative Director:
Lisa Rosenthal
Senior Art Director: Delores Swanson
Art Director: Stephanie Michaud
Writers: Dawn Anderson,
Phyllis Galbraith, Linda Neubauer,
Lori Ritter
Editor: Janice Cauley
Researcher/Designer: Michael Basler
Researchers: Linda Neubauer, Lori Ritter
Sample Production Manager:
Carol Olson
Senior Technical Photo Stylist:
Bridget Haugh
Technical Photo Stylists: Sue Jorgensen,
Nancy Sundeen
Styling Director: Bobbette Destiche
Project Stylist: Joanne Wawra
Prop Stylist: Joanne Wawra
Lead Artisan: Carol Pilot
Artisans: Arlene Dohrman,
Phyllis Galbraith, Carol Pilot,
Michelle Skudlarek, Nancy Sundeen
*Vice President of Development Planning
& Production:* Jim Bindas
Director of Photography: Mike Parker
Creative Photo Coordinator:
Cathleen Shannon
Studio Manager: Marcia Chambers
Lead Photographer: Mark Macemon
Photographer: Billy Lindner

Contributing Photographers: Paul Najlis,
Christopher Wilson
Print Production Manager: Patt Sizer
Senior Desktop Publishing Specialist:
Joe Fahey
Desktop Publishing Specialist:
Laurie Kristensen
Production Staff: Tom Hoops,
Jeanette Moss, Mike Schauer,
Mike Sipe, Greg Wallace, Kay Wethern
Shop Supervisor: Phil Juntti
Scenic Carpenters: Troy Johnson,
Rob Johnstone, John Nadeau
Contributors: Design Master;
DMC Corporation; Hill Design Inc.;
Kunin Felt—Division of Foss
Manufacturing Company; Minnetonka
Mills, Inc.; New Basics Limited
(WildFiber™); Westcoast Woodcraft
Supply
Printed on American paper by:
R. R. Donnelly & Sons Co.

02 01 00 99 98 / 6 5 4 3 2

Creative Publishing international, Inc.
offers a variety of how-to books. For
information write:
Creative Publishing international, Inc.
Subscriber Books
5900 Green Oak Drive
Minnetonka, MN 55343